TOLSTOY

THE GUIDES FOR THE PERPLEXED SERIES

Related titles include:

Beckett: A Guide for the Perplexed Jonathan Boulter

Deleuze: A Guide for the Perplexed Claire Colebrook

Derrida: A Guide for the Perplexed Julian Wolfreys

Existentialism: A Guide for the Perplexed Steven Earnshaw

Literary Theory: A Guide for the Perplexed Mary Klages

TOLSTOY: A GUIDE FOR THE PERPLEXED

JEFF LOVE

continuum

Continuum International Publishing Group

The Tower Building	80 Maiden Lane
11 York Road	Suite 704
London SE1 7NX	New York NY 10038

www.continuumbooks.com

British Library Cataloguing-in-Publication Data
A catalogue record for this book is available from the British Library.

ISBN: 978-0-8264-9378-1 (hardback)
978-0-8264-9379-8 (paperback)

Library of Congress Cataloguing-in-Publication Data
A catalogue record of this book is available from the Library of Congress.

Typeset by Newgen Imaging Systems Pvt Ltd, Chennai, India
Printed and bound in Great Britain by MPG Books Ltd, Bodmin, Cornwall

CONTENTS

ACKNOWLEDGMENTS

It is a pleasure to acknowledge the support provided by the College of Architecture, Art and Humanities at Clemson University in the form of a research fellowship that gave me time to work on this book in 2006 and 2007. In addition, I would like to thank the generous scholars whose teaching, advice and questions have shaped my thinking about Tolstoy, including Vladimir Alexandrov, Caryl Emerson, Robert Louis Jackson, Michael Holquist, Inessa Medzhibovskaya, Gary Saul Morson, Donna Orwin and William Todd. I would also like to thank my colleagues at Clemson, Johannes Schmidt and Margit Sinka, who create a congenial atmosphere for carrying out projects such as these, and my students, whose fascination with Tolstoy's great novels testifies generously as to why the latter have won such an exalted place in the modern memory.

NOTE ON DOCUMENTATION
AND TRANSLATION

All references to the Russian text of Tolstoy's works are to the Jubilee Edition, *Polnoe sobranie sochinenii* in 90 volumes (Moscow, 1928–1958), which is still authoritative, although a new Russian collected edition of a planned 100 volumes is currently underway. Since the text of the literary works contained in a later edition, the *Sobranie sochinenii* in 20 volumes (Moscow, 1960–1965), frequently marks an improvement over the Jubilee Edition, I have consulted that text, particularly with regard to *War and Peace*. Throughout the book, references indicate first the relevant volume of the Jubilee Edition, then the chapter of the work (or book, part and chapter as the case may be) followed by the page number in both the Jubilee Edition and the translation listed in the Works Cited. In this latter regard, I have sought to use readily available translations, which I have modified sparingly.

As a final comment, it should be noted that I have kept explicit engagement with scholarly opinion in this book to a minimum since the intended audience reaches well beyond the confines of Tolstoy scholarship. To compensate for this lack, however, I have made considerable efforts to direct readers, where possible through the reference apparatus, to representative interpretations that oppose, or offer a potential critique of, those I advance.

WHAT IS TRUTH?

Why read Tolstoy? The question is perhaps superfluous, inviting a set of handy answers: Tolstoy is a cultural monument, a "classic," a genius, a towering figure of European literature, and so on. But none of these answers supplies an answer; they simply pass the question off to the authority of the ostensibly obvious, the stolidly self-evident that is the bulwark of all refusals to think. And precisely here is a reason to read Tolstoy. For nothing could be more magnificently characteristic of Tolstoy than his stubborn (and, for some, perverse) rejection of the answers so frequently given to the simplest questions, those one might be ashamed even to ask in view of the overwhelming self-evidence stacked up against them. All of his long life, in all of his many works, Tolstoy fought against self-evidence, fought against any authority that dared to impose silence on those who could not but speak, who, to recall one of his memorable late tracts, could not be silent. Yet, at the same time, few could be said to have sought authority more passionately, more violently, and more immoderately. Few could be said to have longed after simplicity, self-evidence, and the end of the terrible tumult of speech with greater zeal and conviction than this same Tolstoy.

Many approaches to Tolstoy have been eager to give a satisfying account of this discrepancy, of the tension between a hunger for and denial of authority. They have strained to classify Tolstoy in some way in order to place him safely in the wax museum of received ideas; they have molded, refined, and corrected him so that his work may be reduced to a series of comfortably consistent positions. Whatever might be glimpsed at the interstices of these positions, whatever might not agree to offer itself within the framework they impose, falls away into the oblivion of the irrelevant or intractable. But it is precisely these interstices that express the difficulty and implacable power of Tolstoy, the subtraction of his work from the grasp of the would-be "master," the interpreter or reader who would impose his or her own will on the text. It is this Tolstoy, a Tolstoy whose texts never fully yield, that I shall endeavor to explore in this book.

I shall do so, moreover, by hewing to a fundamental question, a path of discovery, that Tolstoy embraced and never successfully evaded: What is truth? This question haunts Tolstoy's works in all their prodigious variety, from the earliest stories to the most shrill of his later tracts.[1] While ostensibly straightforward, the question reveals a complex double aspect, which I think useful to outline here.

In English, the use of articles, "a" or "the," allows one to distinguish between "a" truth, truths or "the" truth (of X or Y), and "truth itself." The former refer to particular truths of and within defined contexts, for example, a situation, discipline, or tradition. The latter refers to what must obtain generally of all truths in order for them to be so classified. Tolstoy's works express inquiries into both these aspects of truth, not only seeking to ascertain the truth in regard to a particular situation but also the significance of that truth as affirming, in a far broader sense, the essential characteristics and validity of truth as such. Each particular inquiry contributes thus to a greater, general inquiry into truth.

There is much at stake in this inquiry. For, if the general inquiry into truth fails to identify its quarry, the result may be loss of a coherent basis for our experience of reality, a loss that raises very troubling questions about the nature and purpose of human life. But that is not all. To fail to identify truth may impose yet another truth of its own, namely, that there is no such thing as truth. This statement exhibits a circuitous irony in so far as the search for truth itself directs us to its absence; that far from having a positive nature or identity, truth denotes the irremediable absence of such a nature or identity. The significance of this irony may be clarified by considering the inquiry into truth as a central mode of inquiry into authority.

What is this authority? It is the presence of a basis for our experience of reality that legitimates certain kinds of experience at the expense of others. Truth is the key representation of authority here: for truth is this basis, which stands firm in all situations and from which no deviation is possible if it is not possible as error. Truth offers, then, the fixed mark by which we may successfully direct our affairs, from quotidian demands to the most far-reaching plans.

In this sense truth provides security, the assurance that our lives can be structured in a conclusive way, and it removes the need to think other than to the extent one needs to think about one's obedience to the authority it represents. The converse, living without authority, entails the absence or irrelevance of any fixed mark, a provisionality that can never be overcome. Hence, when truth points firmly to its own absence, the consequences are unsettling because settlement of any kind depends on a decision or judgment that cannot claim to depend on any fixed mark. Whatever one does, one cannot be sure that one is acting rightly in doing so, one is never sure of the consequences, one is simply never sure.

The inquiry into truth is thus at its core about security; to use a commonplace romantic metaphor, it is about finding a shelter or home, a place of rest and respite from the turbulence of change, all such change hinting in some way at the most fearsome of changes, death. Viewed from this perspective, Tolstoy's stubborn inquiry into truth expresses a powerful rebellion against death. For, if the essence of truth is that truth is simply absent, then one may only conclude that impermanence reigns supreme, that there is no secure haven for human beings, no shelter from change, no assurances against death.

Small wonder, then, that Tolstoy was among the most consciously death-driven of great writers.[2] His fundamental faith in death was from all evidence far greater than his faith in the possibility of overcoming death through some truth that could not have arisen other than as a palliative or opiate for the terminal patient we all are. This formidable, terrible struggle to overcome death is a primary generative axis of Tolstoy's explorations and an attempt to respond to the legacy of Greek tragedy, a legacy renewed in every inquiry into truth, in every striving to establish truth as a fortress against the connivance of change and death. For the wisdom of Greek tragic thought embraces a devastating judgment on human life: faced with the suffering that infects our fragile life in the world, one must admit that it would be best not to have been born.

PLAN OF THE BOOK

Throughout this book, I shall investigate Tolstoy's pursuit of truth, as novelist, militant, and sage, largely in terms of his profound grasp of the power of the infinite to disrupt that pursuit. In this regard, one might divide Tolstoy's career into two grand phases, one distinguished largely by untrammeled, if frequently troubled, literary exploration and daring, reflecting an urgent desire to know that he has had few equals in modern literature, the other largely by public retrenchment and retreat from literature, by a violently uneasy acceptance of the most disturbing lessons of his exploratory phase.

This division of Tolstoy's career is hardly new. Indeed, it is a venerable commonplace of the critical tradition: Tolstoy himself was its passionate advocate.[3] From this standpoint it seems appropriate to begin the book provocatively in a now somewhat traditional[4] way with an examination of Tolstoy's biography, and by that I mean precisely the writing of his life, the remarkable self-fashioning, that ceaselessly absorbed his manifold creative energies. Tolstoy became one of the first truly international celebrities, his fame and authority spread far beyond the confines of Russia, as his correspondence amply demonstrates. His death at the train station of Astapovo in 1910 was an international media event. Both the origins of this celebrity and Tolstoy's generally shrewd management of his image merit attention for the light they shed on the central aspirations of his creative energies as well as on his tremendous ambivalence about them. Here the accent on struggle, at once dispassionate and despairing, that characterizes all of Tolstoy's work can be made clear in a usefully synoptic way, allowing me to articulate a guiding structure for my subsequent discussions.

The first among these considers his great novels, the primary source of his enduring fame, and, more generally, Tolstoy's practice of and attitude toward the novel. For the novel is the generic form most readily ascribed to Tolstoy's greatest fictional works; his distrust and adroit manipulation of that form are telling indicia of Tolstoy's particularly urgent desire to find a way of uncovering truth, the bedrock of experience, that does not reduce experience, that leaves nothing excluded, that is not liable to be toppled or corrupted by an impudent and hitherto ignored detail. Tolstoy's novels seek to grasp a whole, the whole of human life, and they reflect on many levels a sense both of the heroic daring and hubristic vanity of such a striving. Above all, Tolstoy's novels are immense theaters of conflict in which the most stubbornly contradictory views come to be expressed and explored.

While Tolstoy wrote three substantial novels and a number of shorter ones, some of which may be more appropriately called novellas, long tales, or stories, I have chosen to deal with a limited and, perhaps, controversial selection. Of the shorter novels I have chosen two particularly popular ones, *The Cossacks* and *Hadji Murat*. These shorter novels fully deserve their popularity and reflect Tolstoy's abiding fascination with the Caucasus. Moreover, they provide intriguing glosses on techniques and themes that the great novels elaborate in magisterial ways, and, hence, I have decided to begin my discussion of Tolstoy's novels with one of them, *The Cossacks*. Of the long novels, I have chosen only the two undeniably great ones, *War and Peace* and *Anna Karenina*, which are also the most influential, widely read, and discussed. The third, *Resurrection*, published roughly 20 years after the completion of *Anna Karenina*, has been largely neglected, never having achieved a status among critics and readers comparable to that of its illustrious predecessors. There are quite a few reasons for this, not the least of which is expressed by the claim that the book is too baldly ideological (as if *War and Peace* and *Anna Karenina* were not!), thus too transparently and dogmatically didactic, too crudely a vehicle of Tolstoy's later beliefs. Whatever the merits of this claim (and they may well be dubious at best), I have decided to perpetuate this neglect in the present book simply on practical grounds.

Many of the fundamental conflicts featured in the great novels emerge also in the relatively confined laboratory of Tolstoy's shorter fiction. I use the term "laboratory" without hesitation because Tolstoy's shorter fiction often seems to serve as a tightly focused and delimited testing ground for positions that are taken up within much more complex and many-sided wholes in the great novels. Thus the shorter fiction offers a disciplined departure from the strains of holistic world-building that mark the great novels and justify their considerable length. I have chosen four important works for this chapter. Each serves as a focal point for a basic thematic concern of Tolstoy's fiction that both receives more concentrated treatment here than in my discussion of the novels and orients my approach to Tolstoy's later activity as a Christian militant. Indeed, all the shorter works I have chosen first appeared in print only after the publication of *Anna Karenina* in 1878, the period typically associated with a major crisis in Tolstoy's life marked by both the rejection of literature (as arrogant and mendacious world-building) and the rise of an ever more pervasive Christian militancy. The themes I address are death, sex, evil, and inequality. The works that focus on them (in that order) are: *The Death of Ivan Ilyich*, *The Kreutzer Sonata*, "How Much Land Does a Man Need?" and *Master and Man*.

While it is certainly and trivially true that other choices could have been made as to theme and that more than one work deals with the themes chosen, my choice is by no means arbitrary. Rather, it follows from two overriding considerations: prevalence of the theme in Tolstoy's work and radicality of fictional treatment. For Tolstoy's late short works are frequently of an unequalled radicalism. They take fiction to the very brink of disaster and manage to do so by approaching themes that threaten the fictional compact, that put in question the adequacy of fiction to the theme at hand. In this sense, Tolstoy's late short works radicalize the battle with silence that is a crucial aspect of the fictional enterprise in all its many manifestations. And that is why I have chosen appropriately "limit" themes that put the question very squarely as to what may justify fiction or as to why speech may be preferable to silence. This is, after all, the overriding question of Tolstoy's later life. His Christian militancy emerges from a fundamental rejection not only of fiction as ideologically unhindered exploration but of the power of language to forge and shape a life. The problem of teaching, one latent in almost all of Tolstoy's work, comes to the fore: How does one find and convey truth, by word or deed? And how does one convert the former to the latter?

This question gains tremendous urgency in Tolstoy's Christian writings and in his more overtly philosophical works. Hence, as a suggestive counterweight to the essentially literary focus of this book, I devote two short chapters to, respectively, a survey of Tolstoy's religious writings and his "antiphilosophy."

Tolstoy's religious writings are voluminous, but, with a few outstanding exceptions, they tend to receive scant attention in more contemporary treatments of his work, mainly because of Tolstoy's overwhelming authority as a literary artist of the very first rank. Still, these writings exercise a fascination all their own. They develop a demanding Christian faith, having roots both in early Christian "anarchism" as well as in the preoccupation with decay that marks the latter half of the nineteenth century in Europe.[5] My discussion of Tolstoy's religion dwells on the connections it shows with his fiction and on how Tolstoy labors to supplant his fictional efforts with a commanding reinterpretation of some of their defining themes.

An important aspect of this reinterpretation is reflected in Tolstoy's ambivalent attitude toward philosophy. On the one hand, Tolstoy is always somewhat of a rationalist, a characteristic expressed most forcefully in his utopian philosophical treatise, *On Life*. On the other hand, Tolstoy's frustration with the limits of reason undermines his philosophical zeal. His late work, *What is Art?*, shows this particularly well. Generally and unsurprisingly classified as a work on aesthetics or, perhaps, on the philosophy of art, I claim that *What is Art?* sets out a polemic against philosophy that is every bit as powerful and militant a rejection of the discursivity inherent in and essential to philosophy as one can find in nineteenth-century Russia or, for that matter, in any of Tolstoy's novels. Indeed, one has to look forward to the early Wittgenstein, upon whom Tolstoy exerted a powerful and lasting influence, to find a similarly polemical account of the impossibility of philosophy, of philosophy's irremediable poverty when faced with death and prospects for the "good life."

Wittgenstein is only one notable case of influence, and the last chapter of this study gives a few suggestive examples of Tolstoy's legacy in the twentieth century. The breadth of Tolstoy's influence on diverse aspects of the twentieth century is astonishing, from the representation of war in fiction, to the political deployment, in countries as different as India and the United States, of nonviolent resistance as a strategy of civil disobedience.

AN OMISSION

Mention of Tolstoy's influence raises important questions about which aspects of his legacy are productive and which are not. In this latter connection, I should like to comment briefly on what I have not included in this book as a separate topic of study: Tolstoy's work as a dramatist. Tolstoy wrote a number of plays which have never succeeded in attracting the intensity of attention so frequently lavished on his other literary productions. The reasons for this are by no means straightforward. Those most commonly given suggest that the plays tend to be of inferior artistic quality relative to Tolstoy's other works. Yet not all the plays are considered to be equally inferior in this respect, and it is, in any event, somewhat difficult to discern which criteria are involved in making such a determination. The decisive factor here might well be that the plays seem too freighted with ideological commitments. To some, they seem little more than awkward propaganda pieces for an unacceptably narrow point of view, a judgment which is of interest in itself and which brings up a number of difficult questions about what a work of art can and cannot do.[6]

My own reason for not including the plays reflects a judgment on their productive power, on their afterlife as nodal points of influence and new creation. While Tolstoy's other artistic works continue to engage new audiences and writers throughout the world,[7] while his teachings on nonviolence continue to show their power, if perhaps only indirectly through his influence on Gandhi and Martin Luther King Jr, and while his reservations about philosophy and aesthetics continue to reach sympathetic ears (at least via Wittgenstein's influence), the plays simply do not enjoy such a status. They are seldom performed or read and have had hardly any role in the general development of drama in the twentieth century. If there are reservoirs of yet to be exploited artistic potential in the plays—and this is surely a question that admits of no clear response at the present time—it is outside the purview of this book to demonstrate that they do.

CHAPTER 1

"WHO AM I?"

FLIGHT AND DEATH

Count Lev Nikolaevich Tolstoy died of pneumonia at 5 minutes after 6 in the morning on November 7, 1910.[1] He lay on a simple iron bed in the stationmaster's cottage near the tiny railway station for the hamlet of Astapovo. He was some 320 kilometers from his estate and home, Iasnaia Poliana, where he had been born 82 years before and had spent the greater part of his life. He had left his estate in haste and secrecy 11 days earlier with several possible destinations in mind, but he had not found it easy to decide on any one. He was in full flight after all, a fugitive from his wife of 48 years, Sofya Andreevna.[2] While she had now finally caught up to him, she had been confined to a special train languishing on a siding track and was expressly forbidden to see the old man for fear of disturbing him in his delicate condition. She saw him finally only after he had lost consciousness for good. And then she cut a pathetic figure among the others assembled in the room who had striven to exclude her during the dying man's descent into unconsciousness: a troop of doctors, her son Sergei L'vovich, her daughter Alexandra L'vovna (Sasha), and her husband's dear friend, foremost disciple and her bitter opponent, Vladimir Chertkov. Was this depressing scene not a fittingly tragic death for a man who, as Pietro Citati writes, was "pursued by the Furies as few writers in a century when the Furies had reawakened from their sleep?"[3] Or was this death just a piece of grotesque farce, a horrifically trite melodrama with which to end a remarkably fecund life? Or did it contain elements of both? The 11 days leading up to his death offer ample evidence with which to answer each question in the affirmative.

Imagine an 82-year-old man, unable to sleep soundly, beset by anxieties about his wife's unceasing intrusions into his private affairs, his letters, and "secret" diaries. These intrusions had become ever more violent and unpleasant. Sofya Andreevna suspected that Chertkov was conspiring to convince her husband to relinquish the rights to his works and thus leave the children without a major source of income. The polar extremes of Tolstoy's later life are clearly in evidence here: Must he continue to live surrounded by family, luxury, and the rituals of his aristocratic heritage, his life with Sofya Andreevna, or should he live at last according to the ideals of Christian simplicity and humility that he has advocated publicly since his "spiritual rebirth" in the 1880s, his life with Chertkov?

By late October 1910 the conflict between these extremes has reached fever pitch. No one knows peace in the Tolstoy household. There are hysterical scenes, a draining succession of discordant moments. On October 28, Tolstoy hears rustling in his office late in the night and knows that his wife is rifling through his papers once again. He tries to sleep but cannot, so he lights a candle. Seeing light in his room, his wife comes by to check on him. He assures her that he is alright. But nothing could be further from the truth. His heart racing, his tolerance utterly spent, he decides it is time to leave once and for all, time to liberate himself from her watchful care—a kind of care that has become an oppressive, unrelenting surveillance—and from the life of aristocratic luxury that has become too shameful for him, the eloquent enemy of his own class. He quickly rouses himself and writes this condescending letter of farewell to her:

My departure will sadden you. I regret this, but understand and believe that I could not have done otherwise. My position at home is becoming—has become—intolerable. Aside from everything else, I can no longer live in the conditions of luxury in which I used to live and am doing what old people of my age usually do: they withdraw from worldly life in order to live out the last days of their lives in solitude and quiet.

Please understand this and don't come after me if you find out where I am. Your arrival will only worsen your position and mine: it will not change my decision. I thank you for your honorable 48-year life with me and ask you to forgive me for whatever wrongs I have done you just as I forgive you with all my heart for those wrongs that you may have done me. I advise you to reconcile yourself to the new position in which my departure places you and to bear no ill-will towards me. If there's something you should want me to know, tell Sasha: she will know where I am and will send along to me what needs to be sent along; but she cannot tell you where I am because I've made her promise not to speak of this to anyone.

Lev Tolstoy

28 October

I've instructed Sasha to collect my manuscripts and things and send them along to me. (84:404)

After finishing the letter around 4 o'clock in the morning, Tolstoy awakens his personal doctor, Dushan Makovitsky, and Sasha. He arranges for horses and a carriage, has his few things packed and, growing impatient lest Sofya Andreevna awake, rushes out of the house with his customary rapidity. But it is still so dark (5 o'clock in the morning) that he cannot see at all well. He falls into some bushes, hitting a tree and losing his hat. He returns to the house, Sasha gives him a new hat, and he starts on his way again. Accompanied only by Makovitsky, he is soon off in a carriage to the local train station at Shchokino and has to wait a good hour and a half for a train. Where does he want to go? In the long run, he is still not sure. But his first stop will be the famous Optina Pustyn monastery[4] located roughly nine miles from Shamardino, the convent where his sister Marya Nikolaevna, his last surviving sibling, has decided to spend her final years. He wants to see her; only after this visit will he move on to an as yet unspecified place. Having had a long and apparently moving conversation with his sister, Tolstoy considers spending the remainder of his days in the village of Shamardino and even makes arrangements to rent a peasant cottage in the vicinity. But he still fears that his dread pursuer, Sofya Andreevna, may lose control of herself and try to find him at any cost. His fears are not without justification, for Sofya Andreevna has been the center of events at Iasnaia Poliana, events that Tolstoy seems almost too eager to learn about, given his desire to free himself from his old life.

A disciple bearing instructions from Chertkov first tells Tolstoy of Sofya Andreevna's extreme reaction to his departure, including a theatrical attempt at suicide by drowning herself in a relatively shallow pond and various forms of self-mutilation, such as stabbing herself with scissors. She is saved from serious harm in the first instance and scarcely hurts herself severely enough to warrant medical treatment in the second. She remains in a state of hysteria, torn between two vastly different emotional registers, one expressing a profound sense of horror at having driven her husband away, the other an equally profound rage at his having been so bold and childish as to leave her.

Tolstoy responds with sadness to the news, but his resolve remains firm. He cannot go back. This resolve is further tested by the arrival of Sasha at Shamardino on October 30. Sasha brings largely unsympathetic letters from the family, which has gathered in the meantime, together with a letter from Sofya Andreevna pleading for Tolstoy to return. Her pleading is wasted. Agitated and tired, Tolstoy drafts a letter in reply that leaves no room for doubt:

> A meeting between us and, more to the point, my return, are *now* completely impossible. For you, they tell me, this would be harmful in the highest degree, while for me this would be horrible since my condition, as a result of your nervous excitability, your agitated and unhealthy state, would grow even worse, if that were only possible. I advise you to reconcile yourself to what has happened, to adjust to your new position, and, most importantly, to heal yourself.
>
> If you don't really love me, but only don't hate me, you should put yourself in my position if only a little. And if you do that, you will not only not judge me, but you will try to help me find tranquility (*pokoi*), the possibility of some kind of human life, by gaining control of yourself; then you yourself will not wish for my return. But your current mood, desire and attempts to commit suicide, show more than anything else your loss of control over yourself, and they make my return unthinkable. No one but you can free me and, most importantly, yourself from the sufferings felt by all those close to you. Try to put all your energy not into those things which you desire—right now my return—but into calming yourself, your soul, and you will receive what you wish.
>
> I have spent two days at Shamardino and Optina and I am getting ready to leave. I will send a letter while on my way. I am not saying where I will go because I consider separation necessary for you and for me. Don't think that I left because I don't love you. I love you and regret with all my heart that I cannot proceed otherwise. Your letter—I know that it was written sincerely, but you are not capable of doing what you would like to do. And the

matter is not about doing whatever I might want or demand, but only about your stability, a peaceful, reasonable relation to life. As long as there is nothing of the sort, life with you is unthinkable for me. To return to you when you're in such a state would mean for me a refusal to live. And I don't think I am in a position to do that. Good-bye, dear Sonya, may God help you. Life is not a joke, and we've no right to throw it away at will; to measure it by duration is also foolish. Perhaps, the months left to us to live are more important than all the preceding years, and it's necessary to live them well. (84:407–8)

L. T.

Although Tolstoy then tries to rest, he is uneasy. Sasha's arrival has only further exacerbated his fears about Sofya Andreevna's desire to find him. With sudden resolution, he believes that it is time to move on despite mounting and ominous signs of extreme fatigue: it is 3 o'clock in the morning of October 31. He leaves Optina Pustyn early without even having said good-bye to his sister. Tolstoy's destination remains unspecified, but he has grown so weak that he is unable to travel any further than Astapovo station. There Makovitsky decides that it is time to take Tolstoy, who is now shivering and feverish, out of the train. He is helped out of the train by Makovitsky and manages to find a place to sit in the station (the ladies' room), having politely tipped his hat to the many passengers who recognize him. The congenial stationmaster has a bed made up for Tolstoy in his cottage, which is located across from the station.

For a while Tolstoy's condition seems to improve, but his fever soon rises again, and he begins to lapse into various forms of delirium. In this state he has become the absorbing focus not only of his fractious family but of the entire world. News of his flight has spread so fast and far that by November 4 he is in the midst of what one would refer to nowadays as a "media circus." There are up-to-the-hour reports on his condition: everyone enjoys the piquant drama that Tolstoy's waning life has become, complete with hysterical wife and distraught family peering into the cottage to get a glimpse of him since, with the exception of his son Sergei and daughter Tania, they are otherwise forbidden entrance to his room. Moreover, the authorities, fearing the outbreak of violence or even revolution—such is the power Tolstoy wields in Russia at this time[5]—arrange for a vastly increased police presence not only around Astapovo but also in the big cities as well. Protests have broken out in St Petersburg, the country is in a state of restive suspense, and all of this because a desperate old man has tried to escape the too tight bonds of his prior life.

The last few days of Tolstoy's life present a depressing and not infrequently grotesque spectacle more appropriate to a narrative by his great rival, Fyodor Dostoevsky (whose *Brothers Karamazov* Tolstoy had been reading at home the night of his flight and which he had requested Sasha to bring to him at Optina Pustyn)—I shall not give an account of them here.[6] It is perhaps enough to say that, far from finding a place of quiet and solitude, Tolstoy's final days provide a signal example of a new kind of celebrity, an international one, of which he is among the first. His death is swallowed by those forces of modern spectacle and commodification that he most railed against and feared, the very forces that were to wipe away forever the world into which he had been born and whose venerable traditions he had defined in his works as no one before or since.

Tolstoy's outrageous, despairing flight to freedom ends at Astapovo with his entrapment, surrounded by a quarreling family and international media, and under the watchful and concerned eye of the Tsar. The peace he so earnestly sought comes at last only in a ghastly, ironic way, for the unspecified place he reaches in his flight is ultimately the one he has always feared most: death, the "undiscovered country," that fearsome "*it*" of which he writes so powerfully in *War and Peace*.

TOLSTOY'S LIFE

Like so many other aspects of Tolstoy's life, his final days give rise to puzzlement: What kind of life led up to this final catastrophe? What beginnings led to this end? Who was Lev Tolstoy? I should like to respond to these questions by considering Tolstoy's life from two essentially distinct viewpoints, one framed by Tolstoy himself and one relying on the personal observations of two important younger contemporaries—Maksim Gorky and Ivan Bunin, gifted writers each—who came to know Tolstoy late in his life. Specifically, I should like first to set out some of the more significant biographical details of Tolstoy's life, within the initial context of his own attempts to interpret it, before moving on to discuss how these writers assessed his personality. By proceeding in this manner, I hope to provide both a condensed account of Tolstoy's life and an evaluation of just what kind of cultural figure he was as evidenced by two very able and astute contemporaries.

One of Tolstoy's most distinctive characteristics was his relentless drive to classify things. Here drive was met by talent: the precision and clarity of his classifications are astounding, perhaps not to be surpassed. In the words of the eminent historian of ideas, Sir Isaiah Berlin, Tolstoy ". . . saw the manifold objects and situations on earth in their full multiplicity; he grasped their individual essences, and what divided them from what they were not, with a clarity to which there is no parallel" (48). This powerful drive to classify is quite apparent in his later life as he sought a meaningful division of his life into periods. But also apparent here, and perhaps of even greater importance, is Tolstoy's concern to identify underlying patterns, to grasp a life not simply as a haphazard agglomeration of experiences, but as emblematic of an underlying framework, a hidden master narrative by which the apparent muddle of experience may ultimately be clarified, purified of confusion. That Tolstoy sought such a master narrative in regard to his own life is not surprising; this search is one of the principal themes of his greatest fictional creations. The frustration to which this search leads in his fictional works, forcing an ever wider and more varied investigation into the strata of human possibilities, is reflected in the fact that Tolstoy could not decide on one final periodic classification for his own life. He considered several.[7]

Of these the simplest for our purposes is likely the division of his life into four periods that Tolstoy prepared in 1903. This division is also of interest because it originates in a request from Tolstoy's early biographer, Pavel Biriukov, and is preceded by a characteristically ambiguous account of the nature of biography, and of autobiography in particular, as a way of setting out the truth of one's life. Tolstoy's skepticism about autobiography is based primarily on the assumption that it is only natural for us to want to hide the ugly sides of our life, to cleanse our past of those stains that we wish ardently to forget. He writes apropos of Biriukov's request:

I very much wanted to fulfill his request, and in my imagination I started to construct my biography. At first, unbeknownst to myself, I began to recall in the most natural manner only the good things in my life, adding only as shadows of this goodness the dark and bad sides and actions of my life. But considering the events of my life more seriously, I noticed that such a biography would be a lie—although not a direct one—as a consequence of the inaccurate emphasis and portrayal of the good and the silence about, or smoothing over of, the bad. Once I did think about writing the whole honest truth, hiding nothing of the wickedness of my life, I became horrified at the impression such a biography would produce. (34:345)

While this paragraph expresses doubts about autobiography that have many precedents, not the least in scornful criticisms of Rousseau's famous claim in his *Confessions* to reveal the totality of his life regardless of its iniquity,[8] the hesitations are genuinely Tolstoyan, giving some idea of why he was unable to complete the project of autobiography he had set for himself in response to Biriukov. It is difficult to avoid the impression that Tolstoy remains silent about many things, and this is of particular irony since he wrote so very much about himself, as his voluminous diaries attest. But, according to one of the most important critics of his work, Boris Eikhenbaum, the diaries—or, at least, the early ones—function less as a venue of confession than as a sort of laboratory in which the young Tolstoy experimented with techniques of analysis and representation of consciousness that would emerge in his fictional works.[9] Eikhenbaum's observation points to a more intriguing aspect of Tolstoy's autobiographical writings: that they have an intimate relation with his fiction.

In this respect, there is a telling alternation between work on his diaries and work on his fiction. Tolstoy wrote in his diaries primarily when he was not engrossed in his major fiction. During the five years of concentrated work on *War and Peace*, for example, Tolstoy almost completely stopped keeping a diary, only taking it up again when he was blocked or frustrated with the novel's progress. This alternation in turn brings up a tricky and venerable question concerning the line that we may be permitted to draw between fiction and truth, *Dichtung und Wahrheit*, in Tolstoy's writings,[10] a line whose significance becomes clear if we consider the issue in terms of deliberate self-fashioning. For the greatest lie in autobiography is not due to our failure to provide a full account because we do not want to or involuntarily repress aspects of our lives that do not fit the picture we have of ourselves, but to our requiring such a picture in the first place, one shaped in large part by the conventions of narrative appropriate to fiction.

In this broader sense, is not every act of self-representation a betrayal or lie by its very nature? Could it be otherwise?[11]

That Tolstoy was acutely aware of this problem is suggested by one of his favorite poems, Fyodor Tiutchev's *Silentium*, a prominent line of which is: "the spoken thought is a lie." This line in turn has its correlate in a noteworthy aphorism of Stendhal (Henri Beyle), another author whom Tolstoy greatly admired—"every powerful man lies as soon as he speaks and even more so when he writes."[12] What is at stake here? On the one hand, if we claim that the relation between Tolstoy's autobiographical writings and his fictional undertakings is much less clearly defined as one of truth to fiction, then we offer up room for interpreting Tolstoy's autobiographical writings as a specific kind of fictionalization with complex ties to what has generally been accepted as his fictional work proper. In this respect, Tolstoy's autobiographical writings may be interpreted with justice as a sophisticated form of self-fashioning. On the other hand, if we claim that Tolstoy's autobiographical works are the trans-(not de-)scription of a life, then the integrity of the division between autobiography and fiction is easier to maintain, saving reality from the largely unwelcome and idiosyncratic incursion of imagination.

Many of Tolstoy's admirers would shrink at the first possibility: the "great writer of the Russian land,"[13] the writer who violently attacked all forms of artifice, of inauthenticity, could not possibly be guilty of making a fiction of his own life other than inadvertently or unconsciously. For them another, rather less naïve, Tolstoy cannot exist. Moreover, to declare that such a Tolstoy does exist is to play Judas to the deepest currents in Tolstoy's thought, those expressing without qualification a reverence for the world in its immediate and unavoidable "thereness." But thinking of this ilk is itself captive to nostalgia for such immediacy, for some sort of preconceptual (or prelinguistic) bedrock of experience; it thereby misses the formidably protean energies of Tolstoy's creative impulse, remaining within the enchanted circle of a long discredited empiricism that Tolstoy never tires of ridiculing when it suits his purpose. A far more likely or, at least, even-handed supposition might be that Tolstoy moves at once in both directions, as he so often does elsewhere, affirming the (largely positivist, empiricist) prejudices of his age as to what constitutes reality while also leaving behind enough tracks so that these prejudices end up being undermined or fatally weakened. In this respect,

Tolstoy's writings are all of a piece, maintaining boundaries between reality and fiction while, at the same time, suggestively blurring them by a subtle, self-conscious devotion to form, to approaching life as a project of classification or *formation*.[14]

Tolstoy's division of his formation into four parts is worth reproducing:

> Recalling my life in this spirit, that is, examining it from the point of view of the good and evil I have done, I saw that my life can be broken down into four periods: 1) that marvelous and—especially in comparison with what was to come—innocent, joyful and poetic period from childhood up to 14 years old; then the second, terrible period of foul debauchery, of servitude to vainglory, vanity and, above all, to lust; then the third period of some 18 years from my marriage up to my spiritual birth, which may be called moral from a worldly point of view, since during those 18 years I led a correct and honorable family life, not succumbing to any vices condemned by public opinion, but limiting all my interests to egotistical concerns for family, increase of wealth, obtaining literary success and all manner of satisfactions.
>
> And, finally, the fourth 20-year period in which I am currently living and in which I hope to die and from whose standpoint I see the whole meaning of my past life and which I do not wish to change in any way except in regard to those evil habits which were acquired by me in the earlier periods. (34: 346–7)

There are several characteristically Tolstoyan elements in this quadripartite division: the privileging of innocence, the horror both at lusts of the flesh and of the spirit, and the tendency, as noted above, to strive for a final purpose that explains how all actions in a life fit together. But this is only the surface, and when we look at the established facts of Tolstoy's life (as well as a few apocryphal ones), a somewhat different life comes into view that hints at the inadequacy of classification. Let's start with the rawest of facts, using Tolstoy's quadripartite division as a backdrop.

He was born at Iasnaia Poliana on August 28, 1828 to Count Nikolai Ilyich Tolstoy and his wife Marya Nikolaevna, née Volkonskaia. He was the fourth of five children, with three elder brothers, Nikolai, Sergei, and Dmitrii, as well as a sister, Marya, two years younger. His parents belonged to ancient and distinguished aristocratic houses, the estate of Iasnaia Poliana being part of his mother's dowry. Only a few months after the birth of Tolstoy's sister, his mother died. He thus barely knew her, although by all accounts his attempts at remembering or creating her were of great importance to the picture of his childhood he cultivated. His father was distant, this being quite typical for aristocratic families of that era, and died when Tolstoy was barely 9 years old. In contrast, Tolstoy's intimacy with, and feeling for, his brothers was strong and durable. A striking memory that seemed to gain importance as Tolstoy grew older concerned the so-called "ant brotherhood" that his brothers concocted, a sort of religious brotherhood dedicated to universal harmony and well-being. In this connection, a charming Tolstoyan legend has it that Tolstoy's eldest brother, Nikolai, the chief "ant brother," insisted that the secret of creating earthly happiness for all was written on a green stick buried in a ravine at Iasnaia Poliana, and the supposed location of this stick is where Tolstoy asked to be and was buried in 1910. After their father's death, the orphaned children were placed under the guardianship of their father's pious and eccentric sister, Countess Aleksandra Ilyinichna Osten-Saken, but a distant relative, Tatiana Aleksandrovna Ergolskaia, assumed the primary responsibilities for taking care of them. Countess Aleksandra died only four years later in 1841, and the children were entrusted to her sister Pelageia, who lived in Kazan as the wife of a prominent local landowner. The children were thus uprooted from Iasnaia Poliana to Kazan, some 600 kilometers east of Moscow, and Tatiana Ergolskaia, by now Tolstoy's beloved "Aunt Toinette," was forced to stay behind. Against this back-drop of death and separation, the second period of Tolstoy's life began with an event that seems to seal the end of his "joyful" childhood: losing his virginity to a prostitute at the tender age of 14.

Now commenced for Tolstoy a time of daring in which he distinguished himself in many of the chief aristocratic arts, hunting, whoring, gambling, and warfare, all the while struggling against himself, what he considered his too dissolute, indolent, and animal nature. He was by turns shy and impossibly haughty, withdrawn and gregarious, gently sentimental and violent—the Tolstoy of legend, the always unexpected and contradictory personality, came to the fore in these years. He was constantly exploring, trying to find how destiny intersected with his life, to determine what he was meant to be; for he firmly believed that he was not of the common run. Yet, at the university of Kazan, he was a fitful, inconstant student, hardly a promising one, and he never received a degree. This meager student effort was hardly unusual in a time when students often did not take degrees and in an empire where the total number of students (out of a population of some 60 million) did not exceed several thousand. He seems to have much preferred gambling, drink, and women to his studies; it is thus not surprising that he suffered his first bout of venereal disease at this time and had to spend several weeks alone in the university clinic. This is when he began the "Franklin" diary he was to keep for the rest of his life. His first efforts at describing himself, which, as Eikhenbaum argued, were the first steps on his literary path, emerged in response to venereal disease, surely an interesting conjuncture.[15] By 1847 he had come into his inheritance and he left the university to return to Iasnaia Poliana. For the next few years he lived an unsettled life, wintering in Moscow and St Petersburg. He amassed such threatening gambling debts that his brothers thought well of his leaving with Nikolai for the Caucasus in 1851. This trip initiated a new stage in his life, that of the warrior, which lasted for the first half of the 1850s. While he was, strictly speaking, merely an observer at first, he soon gained a commission, was promoted twice, fighting bravely in the Caucasus and then in the Crimean war, where he distinguished himself at the siege of Sebastopol. He also began writing in earnest, publishing several literary works, *Childhood* (1852), that depicted a childhood very much like his own, "The Raid" (1852), an outstanding war tale, and his celebrated *Sebastopol Sketches* (1855–1856), which in their power and economy of description, have exercised a great influence on many writers among whom Ernest Hemingway is one of the notables. Upon retirement from military service in 1856, he returned to St Petersburg where he was feted by the literary celebrities of the day and even lived with the most esteemed among them, Ivan Turgenev. While Tolstoy's literary success flattered him, he despised the literati and did his level best to shock the gentle Turgenev. He visited Europe twice, once in 1857 and again in 1861. On the first trip he witnessed an execution in Paris that profoundly disturbed him.[16] On his second trip he met with a variety of important figures such as Matthew Arnold and Pierre-Joseph Proudhon; he wanted to educate the peasant children on his estate and sought out first-hand information about the latest European methods. Disillusioned, he settled back into Iasnaia Poliana, with his peasant school and dear Aunt Toinette.

Although he had not yet curtailed his aggressive sex life—he was in fact involved in a passionate love affair with the wife of one of his peasants—he increasingly longed to get married. The next major period of his life began with this marriage. Sofya Andreevna (née Behrs) was 18 years his junior. She was intrigued by Tolstoy's strangeness, which took on other shades when, after their engagement had been assured, he handed her his diaries. While this was not an unusual thing to do at the time, it was also not very prudent, for, once Sofya Andreevna learned the details of Tolstoy's affairs, she was disgusted, and it is perhaps remarkable that she did not repudiate him. They soon were married and moved to Iasnaia Poliana where Sofya Andreevna learned that one of the house serfs—the woman mentioned above—was now pregnant by her husband. Sofya Andreevna managed to adjust to this and to the tedium of life in the country, a hard prospect for a girl brought up in Moscow society as the daughter of an eminent doctor. From 1863 on came a succession of children, 13 in all, of whom 8 survived into adulthood. This period is also the high noon of Tolstoy's literary creativity; having published *The Cossacks* in 1863, he started writing a new work that would become *War and Peace* (1869). The first shadows of crisis appeared after the completion of *War and Peace* with an eerie experience of death at an inn in Arzamas that was of enduring significance for Tolstoy, so much so that he wrote an account of it, *Confessions of a Madman,* almost 20 years later. In the early 1870s Tolstoy cast about and finally fastened onto the rudiments of a new novel (apparently after reading a story fragment by Pushkin, called "The guests were arriving at the country house . . .")[17] that became *Anna Karenina* and was to occupy the remainder of the decade, coming out in book form first in 1878.[18] Tolstoy went through a period of prolonged crisis after finishing *Anna Karenina,* and it is around this time that Tolstoy's "spiritual birth" seems to have taken place.

This birth, inaugurating the fourth and final period of his life, was introduced by the stark and powerful work, *A Confession* (1881), which heralds a radical Christian militancy coupled with repudiation of his past works and life. As a Christian militant renouncing his own class, Tolstoy grew famous around the world and wielded such authority that, as we saw at Astapovo, the Tsar himself was hesitant to move against him for fear of public opprobrium. But, for all that, Tolstoy did not simply stop writing literary works, although his public attitude toward literature was often harsh and condemnatory. Indeed, he produced during this period an immense variety of different kinds of writing that has arguably not yet been adequately examined or classified. He wrote novels, short stories, plays, tales for children, a commentary and consolidation of the four gospels, works of philosophical and theological speculation, polemical inter-ventions in major events of the day as well as maintaining his diaries (to be sure, with interruptions), and an enormous correspondence. The major works of this period are thus quite various, one long novel, *Resurrection* (1899), two shorter ones, *Hadji Murat* (1896–1904) and *The Forged Coupon* (1902–1904), a sequence of shorter narratives such as *The Death of Ivan Ilyich* (1886), "How Much Land Does a Man Need?" (1886), *The Kreutzer Sonata* (1889), *Master and Man* (1895), and *Father Sergius* (1898); philosophical works such as *On Life* (1887) and *What is Art?* (1898); religious works of various kinds such as *The Gospel in Brief* (1881), *What I Believe* (1883), and *The Kingdom of God Is Within You* (1893); polemical works such as *I Cannot Be Silent* (1908); and, finally, a series of plays such as "The Living Corpse" (1891) and "The Fruits of Enlightenment" (1900).

Tolstoy's Christian militancy reached a certain apogee with his excommunication from the Orthodox Church in 1901. His followers were persecuted, his domestic conflicts emerged more frequently and in thornier form. Tolstoy's last years illustrate how the prolonged enmity between his wife and Chertkov turned into a major conflagra-tion in his life that was resolved decisively by the escape attempt ending at Astapovo.

What do these "facts" tell us? Does Tolstoy not remain simply "enigmatic," in the words of Gorky, "the most enigmatic man of the 19th century?"

TOLSTOY AS CULTURAL ICON

How does one take the measure of a man like Tolstoy, particularly if one has access only to the seasoned celebrity? Gorky's *Reminiscences of Lev Tolstoy* stands out because it seeks to reveal the cunning master of fictions behind the image of the pious man of God, the irrepressibly creative, curmudgeonly and defiant spirit or *daemon* Tolstoy was never able to hide completely. Here Gorky wants to shed light on another Tolstoy who is more like a god himself. He remarks that Tolstoy "looks like a god—not the Lord of Hosts or some

Olympian deity, but the old Russian god that 'sits on a maple throne under a golden linden tree.' Not terribly majestic, but probably more cunning than all the other gods" (32).

The accent on cunning is crucial, still fresh and provocative, and it points to Tolstoy as a man of masks behind which lies a dispassionate, withering gaze on human affairs, a gaze that Gorky can only describe indirectly. Hence, Gorky emphasizes silence, that Tolstoy kept his own counsel about many things and could even be playful or capricious about what he was willing to impart to those around him. There is an especially interesting passage in the *Reminiscences* worth citing in support of this contention:

> I once asked him, "Do you agree with Pozdnyshev when he says that doctors have killed, and are killing, hundreds of thousands of people?"
> "And is that something that interests you very much?"
> "Very."
> "Then I won't tell you!"
> And he grinned and twirled his thumbs. (49)

And then:

> If he were a fish he would of course swim only in the ocean, never visiting the inland seas, especially not the fresh water of rivers. Here he is surrounded by schools of freshwater fish who find what he says neither interesting nor useful, but his silence doesn't frighten or touch them. And he is a master of the impressive silence, like a real hermit who shuns the things of this world. Though he talks a good deal on topics which he feels obliged to discuss, one still senses that there are many more topics on which he keeps silent. There are things one tells to no one. He no doubt has thoughts that frighten him. (38)

What emerges, then, is an interpretation of Tolstoy that eschews one sort of myth-making, that of Tolstoy himself and his disciples, in favor of another that picks out the fluid, equivocal, and essentially pagan aspects of Tolstoy. While Gorky seems to draw on some of the oldest romantic clichés regarding the artist, he also moves beyond them in so far as he finds a Tolstoy for whom the role of religious prophet or elucidator would seem ridiculous or naive, hence, a Tolstoy who is quite aware of both the frailty and necessity of faith.

This Tolstoy is in sharp contrast to the one Bunin sets out in his *Liberation of Tolstoy*. While Bunin is just as taken by the grandeur of the man as Gorky, he works hard not to grant Tolstoy god-like mythic status. Bunin's Tolstoy is a troubled seeker, a double of the indefatigable seekers of the major novels, and his object is freedom, liberation from the confining limitations of this life. In other words, Bunin's Tolstoy is a powerfully human character, a restless victim of dissatisfaction, who is unable to find any way out of that dissatisfaction and yet is condemned to try. This Tolstoy is definitely not a god, but a man, not the author of a world like that created in *War and Peace*, but one who, like the author of *Anna Karenina*, despairs of the possibility of such creation, of the stability of the human.

Faust and Buddha are the opposing extremes Bunin astutely invokes in his attempt to define the limits of Tolstoy's personality. The Faustian aspect of Tolstoy is exemplified by the pure ferocity of Tolstoy's desire to master man and animal, to classify, to bring the world to heel by imposing an order upon it. Bunin excels at describing Tolstoy's intensity and strangeness, his piercing eyes and peculiar gait, at once swift and clumsy like that of a gorilla. Tolstoy is shrewd and clumsy, great in his gift of seeing what others cannot see and awkward in his employment of that gift. This awkwardness is not a fault, rather it merely emphasizes the extremity of conflict in Tolstoy between his extraordinary talent and his equally extraordinary ordinariness. Hence, while Bunin eschews the overt myth-making of Gorky, he still draws a portrait of a human being splendidly and disturbingly, if not monstrously, different from others. Bunin is, however, also concerned to convey Tolstoy's valiant attempts to overcome or tame the excesses of his personality, to "empty" himself or be free of attachment, like the Buddha. The composite that results is explicitly and, perhaps, somewhat primitively psychologizing, unearthing deep division between these opposing tendencies, one aggressive, the other quiescent, one expressing a violent will to shape and dominate this earthly life, the other a hope of freedom from such a will, of the attachments to this very same earthly reality.[19]

The common thread in both these accounts of Tolstoy's personality is their recognition of the centrality of unease in Tolstoy, that far from being the serene follower of Jesus, he was a creature of conflict, of perpetual struggle, exemplifying Schelling's famous line that "where there is struggle, there is life."[20]

THE PROBLEM OF THE AUTHOR

The final question that needs clarification for the purposes of this chapter is a decisive one: Why should we concern ourselves with the facts of Tolstoy's life in the first place? This question may offer no difficulty at all. One could say that the biography is purely of secondary interest. After all, the works first create the interest in the man. But why such an interest? Surely, the usual answer to this question has everything to do with widely held notions of an author's authority as expressed in the intention that governs the work. By this I mean the proposition that the guide for distinguishing a good from a bad interpretation of the text lies in determining to what extent an interpreter divines the author's intent and discerns therein the "true" contours of the text upon whose basis one can build an interpretation that has convincingly final authority.

There are a host of problems lurking just beneath the surface of this kind of thinking. While it is not hard to accept the fact that the biography first becomes interesting in connection with the text (although, as one can see from the example of Tolstoy alone, the biography may thenceforth exert its own fascination), the question of authorial intention or authority as a ground for interpretation is a treacherous one. It is treacherous precisely because it is not at all easy to determine what an author's intention is at any given moment of the text. What evidence do we have for that intention other than the text itself? Moreover, if the author makes a subsequent gloss on a portion of the text, should we assume that the portion of text glossed must be read as the author prescribes?

Such respect for authorial intention belongs in fact primarily to the nineteenth century, and it has been vigorously attacked in the twentieth, where its basic assumptions have been called into question. First of all, there is the evidentiary burden mentioned previously: Just how does one ascertain the author's intent? Does one collect outside texts, anecdotes from the biography, and so forth as proof that he or she thought a certain way? Should we apply that way to the text? Is there some formula or series of formulae that guarantee the accuracy of such an approach? Moreover, there is the even more problematic claim that an author conceives of what he or she wants to say and then proceeds to say it: the intention is the text. Yet, who can safely claim to write in such a way that what one wants to say gets said? How does one know what one wants to say at any given time? Even that is an act of interpretation and, since there is no corroborative third party to that act who can see into the mind of the author and reproduce its transactions, the author can never be sure that what he or she sought to express is indeed what was expressed.[21] If this is so, it can only be of equal difficulty for a reader to know what to make of intentions. Rather than a forbidding presence at the core of the text one finds a demanding absence or, what is virtually the same, the impossibility of identifying a conclusive authorial presence in the text that cannot be burned away in the furnace of doubt.[22]

Language is not a mere instrument after all, and it claims far greater control over us than we can claim over it.[23] If, then, the author cannot determine the interpretation of his work, controlling the dissemination of meaning from the grave, what significance can the author have for readers? Not a lot. Or so it may seem. But, in the case of Tolstoy, there is a formidable desire to impose authorial intention on his readers as well as a tacit recognition of the impossibility of doing so. Tolstoy's attempt to merge fiction with his own life is a clear sign of this desire as is his violent attack on critics of art and literature in *What is Art?* Tolstoy sought to appropriate his own works, to ensure that they not escape him and speak differently to different people. Tolstoy seems to hold to the criticism of writing that Plato mentions in the *Phaedrus*, namely, that writing undermines the purity of the spoken word, allowing for a distressingly broad and equivocal range of interpretation: once a text is made public, it can be read in many, many ways.

Hence, Tolstoy's complex attempt to interweave life and works is itself of considerable interest, not only in regard to the assumptions about authorship it implies, but also in regard to the concept of authority that such interweaving at once openly extols and undermines. Here we have yet another version of that attitude to truth that I mentioned in my introductory comments, for Tolstoy seeks to establish an authority and to bring it down. He at once wants to believe but cannot. That this characteristic pattern appears both in his life and works insinuates an intimate relation between the two, a kind of "fictionality" pertaining to both, that denies the ultimate validity of the separation of life and works. More radically, the blurring of borders here puts in question the notion of authority that under-writes the separation between biography and works: each becomes an extension of the other. This complex interplay is perhaps what is most characteristic of Tolstoy where borders are established and destroyed in a continuous tumult, surcease from which is equivalent to death.

CHAPTER 2

A NOVELIST?

TOLSTOY AND THE NOVEL

As *Anna Karenina* began to take shape in the spring of 1873, Tolstoy informed his close friend, philosopher Nikolai Strakhov, that for about a month he had been writing "of all things a novel, the first of my life" (62:25). This is a puzzling admission, coming only four years after the complete publication of *War and Peace* and ten years after the publication of *The Cossacks*, both of which have been considered masterfully executed exemplars of the genre: Is Tolstoy not first and foremost a novelist? Yet, the mere fact that Tolstoy should consider two important works—*War and Peace* being for some his most important—to be something other than novels is indicative of Tolstoy's discomfort with generic classification and, in particular, the primary generic classification applied to his greatest works of fiction. Tolstoy went to considerable lengths to convince his readership that *War and Peace* was not a novel but rather "what the author wished and was able to express in the form in which it was expressed" (16:7), a teasingly obscure formulation that simply deprives the reader of any generic markers with which to guide reading of the work.[1]

Rejection of generic markers is characteristic of Tolstoy's approach to fiction (and of course not only to the novel) whereby he sought to clear away the detritus of convention so as to open up space for a new and "innocent" relation of reader to text not encumbered by ingrained habits of reading. Contrary to his general reputation as a writer who fulfilled the possibilities of a genre rather than overwhelming or renovating it, Tolstoy was in fact an astute formal experimenter who sought to undermine the role of mediating authority. The vaunted realism of Tolstoy owes much of its persuasive power to refined destructive strategies whereby a received approach is unmasked as limited and artificial by another that at one stroke offers what the received approach supposedly cannot while masking its own precarious artifice through an ingenious rhetoric of destructive critique.[2]

Tolstoy's attitude to genre is but one, albeit very important, aspect of a greater enterprise, the net result of which is a tremendous increase in the authority of the Tolstoyan text in its aggressive deviation from the artifices of convention.[3] Precisely in these terms one may count Tolstoy among the most aggressive and tyrannical of writers. It can hardly be mere coincidence that Harold Bloom, effusively praising Tolstoy's talent, places him alongside Homer, Dante, Shakespeare, and the Yahwist writer of Genesis and Exodus, all of whose works impose a *sui generis* authority that expresses the essence of canonic authority for Bloom: the creation of a reality so compelling that it becomes the fabric of everyday life, the inventory of its representational possibilities.[4]

While this judgment fits a common apprehension of Tolstoy, it is by no means conclusive. One has only to look within the major novels themselves to find analogous quests for immediacy, an unencumbered relation to the world. But these analogies are curious and ironic, for frustration distinguishes them. The sought-after goal remains perpetually elusive, at once enticing and haunting. The complexly ramified patterns of seeking apparent in these novels are unified by their common fate, failure, if not by the responses to that common fate. This pattern of frustration has obvious implications for the question of generic classification as the assertion of authority behind the dismissal of generic markers may well be incapable of maintaining itself for more than a brief incandescent moment.

The fundamental problem identified by this pattern of frustration has to do with the impossibility of the mimetic task Tolstoy's fiction appears to set for itself: to portray the world in all its immediacy, to obtain and to communicate truth as a persuasively complete vision of the whole that shares many of the characteristics of divine intuition. Let me quickly unpack this statement, reviewing for the sake of clarity some of the territory I have just covered.

The basic premise of my argument is that Tolstoy's rejection of generic classification for his longer fictions reflects a more general concern with the elimination of mediating interventions, which, in turn, points to a fundamental valorization of immediacy, of an apprehension not limited in any way (for mediating interventions are by their very nature the intrusion of a specific *means* or *mode* of apprehending). Unlimited apprehension is free, undistorted, and complete: it is panoptic and, like its model, divine intuition, an immediate, infinite knowing or capture of all that is *as* it is in its unalloyed purity and particularity.[5] But immediate knowing remains impossible for a human being because human knowing is finite. It is relative to, and hence limited by, a means by which something may be known: human knowing depends on both an origin and an apparatus (basic examples of which are sense perception or language).[6] Merely to claim to portray or communicate immediacy is thus fraught with insuperable difficulties because the necessity for relying on a means to do so abolishes that immediacy.

This problem can be translated into more concrete terms by reference to a central feature of the modern novel, the narrative of discovery or adventure as loss of a certain kind of illusion. From Cervantes' *Don Quixote* (1605) to Balzac's *Lost Illusions* (1837), novels have been preoccupied with the unmasking of holistic or totalizing views of the world as constituting dreadful impostures or forms of charlatanry. It has been argued from several different points of view that the narrative of discovery peculiar to the modern novel represents the overthrowing of a static, hierarchical, and fundamentally complete conception of the world as a whole in favor of a constantly changing, and therefore unfinished, one that is always on the way to an uncertain, indefinitely deferred goal.[7] A crucial element of this overthrow is the recognition of perspective, a profound contingency that gives the lie to those views which, in an attempt to confer on themselves a universal, impersonal authority, an undistorted "view from nowhere"—otherwise known as *the* truth—would have their contingency carefully concealed.

What distinguishes Tolstoy is his concurrent acceptance and rejection of this narrative of discovery, his provocatively nonnovelistic practice of the novel. On the one hand, Tolstoy appears to make both explicit and implicit claims for authority in his novels that seem utterly opposed to the spirit of the novel as a genre which rejects such claims. On the other hand, these claims for authority are always undermined within the novels themselves, this being the central significance of both the striving for immediacy and the necessary failure of that striving as I have tried to describe it. The end result is that Tolstoy's novels represent the world as a question, a space of change and transition between a kind of closed *cosmos*, the picture of the world against which the novel is supposed to direct its narrative inventiveness, and the vertiginous openness that proceeds from inventiveness. This space is the dynamic structural foundation of Tolstoy's novels, articulating itself on all levels with almost infinite subtlety, from the life of a particular character, to the formal peculiarities of the narrative, to the narrator's shifting point of view.

Expressed in terms of the loss of illusions, one might describe this tension in more typically romantic language as revealing an incessantly fluid gap in identity that provides the motive force behind action and, in an exemplary fashion, behind creative action in its various guises. Action is concerned to eliminate this unacceptable gap—unacceptable because the latter exposes our essential finitude and fragility: it is the anonymous, featureless face of death. But, like all human things, action cannot evade its own fragility and is continually vulnerable to attack. Few writers show greater perspicuity with this kind of attack than Tolstoy, and his narratives suggest that the creation and overthrow of fictions that seek to hide or flatter our fragility constitute an unalterable pattern in human life. The only way to escape this circle of despair is not to participate in it. Innocents and masters of renunciation are the ones who may call themselves free in this sense, and their freedom is bought at the cost of avoiding becoming an aware human being, one born to the world.

CASE STUDIES: *THE COSSACKS, WAR AND PEACE, ANNA KARENINA,* AND *HADJI MURAT*

Taking this conceptual network as a basic reference point, I shall examine four important novelistic works by Tolstoy in this chapter. Among these are the two large "loose baggy monsters"[8] for which Tolstoy is best known, *War and Peace* and *Anna Karenina.* But my examination of the two great novels will be preceded by an introductory discussion of *The Cossacks,* the work Tolstoy completed immediately prior to *War and Peace* in 1863, and will end with a discussion of *Hadji Murat,* one of his last works and, for some, his purest, most powerful narrative.[9] These two shorter novelistic works, both dealing with the Caucasus, feature widely differing manners of construction and, in this respect, they offer a suggestive counterpoint to the great novels of Tolstoy's prime, bearing eloquent witness to the considerable changes in Tolstoy's writing which took place over an almost 50-year period.

My approach will not be to provide a comprehensive interpretation of each novel: to do so in the space available would hardly allow
for more than a cursory glance at the incredible complexity of the
large novels and would thus have the effect of a thumbnail sketch
more appropriate to a travel guide than a book designed to tackle the
more difficult aspects of the novels. Rather, I should like to approach
each novel from a particular focal point, a telling aspect of the novel
both revelatory of the work and Tolstoy's novelistic practice. To that
end, I have divided my treatment of the novels into four separate
"studies," which, I hope, will enhance clarity of presentation and ease
of reference.

Study 1: *The Cossacks*

The Cossacks is a book that contains its own counter-book;[10] it is
both a skillfully executed "quest" narrative and a parody of such narratives, both a work with strong affinities to romantic literature and a
polemical assault on the bases of that literature. The plot is admirably simple. A young Russian aristocrat, Dmitri Olenin, bids farewell
to his life of urbane indolence and embarks on a journey to a new,
exotic, and supposedly primitive land, the Caucasus. There he lives
among the Grebensk Cossacks, whose rude traditions he attempts to
make his own. He does not succeed in doing so, however, and returns
to Moscow having realized the utter futility of his efforts. The allegory or generalizing paradigm that emerges from this plot is equally
simple: Olenin's departure for the Caucasus represents the aspiration
for a "return to nature," for a new life freed of the restrictions of
deadening social convention in all its many forms; it represents a
seeking after the immediate and unconditioned, an attempt to live the
world afresh. That this aspiration cannot be fulfilled is the sober conclusion to be deduced from this allegorization of the work.

Such allegorizations are the very lifeblood of romantic literature
and thought. They are exemplary of the kind of irony typically associated with romanticism that consists in pointing out the gap between
aspiration and capability. Hence, the question may arise as to what
extent or in what way *The Cossacks* is really a parody of romantic
literature so understood. The answer to this question has two aspects.
If, on the one hand, the novel tries to show the acute frailty of the
generalizing or allegorizing impulse itself, that experience tends to
undermine our conceptual schemes; on the other hand, it also shows

the vacuity of living in conformity with experience in absence of a conceptual scheme. The counter-book of *The Cossacks* is that contained by all books in the precise sense that the limit of the generalizing or allegorizing impulse is the very silence against which every book raises a form of protest. The novel thus criticizes the goal of romantic striving, not merely in terms of the still romantic pathos that that goal may not be achieved, but, more significantly, by suggesting that achieving it is a form of negation, an expression of the basic paradox that all aspiration strives for its own termination, being a quest for peaceful stasis formally indistinguishable from death.

The space that the novel occupies is, in this respect, fundamentally unsettled: peace or stasis remains out of reach. As long as there is life there is struggle, and Olenin's quest does not end in the novel. Rather, Olenin finds himself wavering at the end, unable to make a determinative choice, even though his final decision to return to Moscow seems to possess that quality.[11] To get an idea of what this choice involves, we need to examine the relation of Olenin to some of the other characters as well as to the natural world he encounters in the Caucasus.

The characters are arranged around Olenin, they constitute his theater of exploration, and his consciousness is one of the primary filters through which we come to know them. They represent for him different possibilities of being, of orienting oneself within the world. This structure is set at the very beginning of the novel where we come upon Olenin with two close friends at a farewell party. In his inimitable way, Tolstoy describes what must be a typical night out for a fairly raffish set of young aristocrats in Moscow. The operative contrast in the opening paragraphs is between these indolent young aristocrats engaged in spirited discussion and working people who, having long been asleep, are just getting up to go off to their work, a useful practical activity:

> Moscow lies silent. From time to time screeching wheels echo in the wintry streets. Lights no longer burn in the windows, and the street lamps have gone out. The ringing of church bells rolls over the sleeping city, warning of the approach of dawn. The streets are empty. The narrow runners of a nighttime sleigh mix sand and snow as the driver pulls over to a corner and dozes off, waiting for a fare. An old woman walks past on her way to church, whose candles, sparse and red, are already burning asymmetrically, throwing their light onto the golden icon stands. The workers of

the city are waking after the long winter night and preparing to go to work.

But fashionable young gentlemen are still out on the town.

Light flickers illegally from behind the closed shutters in one of Chevalier's windows. A carriage, sleighs, and cabs are huddling in a line by the entrance. A mail troika is waiting to leave. A porter, bundled in a heavy coat, stands crouching behind the corner of the house as if hiding from someone.

"Why do they keep blathering, on and on?" a footman sitting in the hall at Chevalier's wonders, his face drawn. (6: I// 3/3)

What do they "keep blathering" about? The young aristocrats are discussing a love affair in which, it seems, Olenin was somewhat unfair. The discussion of love has considerable pertinence to the rest of the novel.[12] The question with which this discussion begins, of whether it is better to love or be loved, recalls the beginning of a famous Platonic dialogue favored by the romantics, the *Phaedrus*. In that dialogue Socrates discusses love, and, in particular, erotic love, outside the walls of Athens with the eponymous main character.[13] There are many interesting aspects of this allusion, but, for our purposes, the most important are likely to be found both in the dialogue's careful exposition of erotic love as a striving whose essence is to return to one's pristine state prior to embodiment and in the fact that this determination is made outside of the city, in the bosom of nature. Let me briefly elaborate these points in the dialogue.

In the *Phaedrus*, Socrates describes an immortal soul that is indestructible and complete, a soul high above the earth, indeed beyond all time and place, that seeks nothing because it lacks nothing. But this soul is liable to corruption as soon as it receives a body, which, leaning slavishly to the earth, cares only for physical satisfaction. Two kinds of love famously emerge in Socrates' account: the love for bodily pleasure and the love for what only the soul can see, namely, the abstract ideas, the forms of things, like "table" or "the good," that are somehow both reflected in and utterly beyond the material world. The former kind of love is base, the latter noble and purifying; it allows an ascent from the ideas as reflected in the material world to the ideas as they are in themselves, eternal and perfect. Here is the governing Western model of education as an erotic ascent from the ever-changing material world of deceptive appearance and becoming to the unchanging ideal world of reality and being. Socrates praises this erotic ascent, which expresses itself as the soul's striving to return home to its prior state of perfection, to encompass the whole as it is in itself by discarding the distortions resulting from emplacement in a body.

The location of the principal discussion between Socrates and Phaedrus outside the city walls invites one to infer that the city must be left behind in order to understand what love is. For love is elemental, "natural," primordial, remaining both prior to and outside the city; it is an originating impulse—here the connection between natural reproduction and the ascent to the ideas is very much evident—whose own nature must be elusive for that very reason. Hence, if the structure of love as a primordial longing is clear, the contents of that longing, its specific instantiation in the material world, may be much more variable.

The allusion, then, identifies Olenin's departure as a complex exploration, as seeking to answer a question not merely about love in a conventional sense, but about love as the pursuit of the highest things, of liberation from the limitations of our mortal state. Moreover, the allusion sets the pattern of this exploration as a return to primordial nature, thus, as a turning away from society—the world created by the city—toward nature defined rudimentarily as what the city is not.

The natural setting is of course the Caucasus. Russian expansion into the region had begun early in the nineteenth century, sparking unrelenting conflict between the Russian military and various opponents, prominent among which were Muslim tribes of Circassia, Chechnia and Dagestan, until the surrender of Shamil, the imam of the Caucasus, in 1859. Olenin is a somewhat belated literary visitor to the Caucasus. Already by the middle of the nineteenth century the region had acquired a dense texture in the Russian imagination and, especially, in literature. Alexander Pushkin, Alexander Bestuzhev-Marlinsky, and Mikhail Lermontov had already written a variety of poems and prose works establishing a largely romantic attitude to the region, an attitude fascinated by rustic simplicity, pliant, exotic beauty, and harsh brutality, all in contrast to the awkward, enervated, ostensibly civilized Russian.[14] The Caucasus had thus acquired a characteristically romantic identity and function within Russian culture, serving as a privileged other against which to measure the achievements and constrictions of Russian society. Here we encounter a form of Russian orientalism barely distinguishable from that cultivated by the other two great empires of Europe, Britain and France.

The Cossacks accepts this cultural heritage mainly as grist for parody. The form of parody that Tolstoy develops in the novel aims not only to reveal weaknesses in one way of representing the Caucasus but also, and more fundamentally, in the act of representation itself. The suggestion not yet fully radicalized in *The Cossacks*—for that radicalization is the glory of *War and Peace*—seems to be that there are things that remain forever beyond representation and which disclose themselves as such, thereby serving as reminders of the limits of what we can bring under our cognitive control.[15] The discrepancy between two different, but mobile, narrative voices is one of the primary sources of these parodic effects in the novel and has puzzled many of its most careful readers.[16] This discrepancy consists in the differing ways in which the narrator and Olenin describe the Cossacks' world. The novel features significant, subtly drawn shifts between what appears to be an "objective" narrative voice and the voice associated with Olenin. The former provides, for example, a brief but magisterial account of Cossack society in chapter IV and maintains a similar tone of sovereign detachment throughout the narrative, thus acting as a putatively firm basis from which to evaluate Olenin's thoughts; not infrequently, this objective narrative voice offers a counterpoint to Olenin's.

Narrative discrepancy thus creates a dissonance which affects many of the important descriptions in the novel. The principal characters arranged around Olenin in the Caucasus, Eroshka, Lukashka, and Maryanka, while enacting a curious repetition of the opening (where Olenin's two friends, one a rival, discuss love for an unnamed woman), all emerge through two lenses. One of the more obvious examples of dissonance concerns Maryanka who becomes the Cossack substitute for the submissive, sloe-eyed Circassian beauty Olenin imagines somewhat lubriciously on his way to the Caucasus. The first description of Maryanka, while acknowledging her beauty, also establishes her role, not as a submissive and seductive creature of Olenin's febrile masculine fantasy, but as someone with simple, and hardly romantic, responsibilities:

> Old Ulitka, the wife of the Cossack cornet and schoolmaster, has come to the gate of her courtyard like many of the other women, and waits for the cattle that her daughter Maryanka is chasing along the road. Before Ulitka can even open the gate, a large, bellowing cow barges into the yard in a cloud of mosquitoes,

followed by well-fed cows trudging slowly, evenly swatting their sides with their tails, their large eyes recognizing Ulitka. Mary-anka, beautiful and lithe, follows the cattle into the yard, throws down her switch, closes the gate, and then hurries on nimble feet to drive the animals into their stalls. (6:V//19/21)

This mild deflation forms a pattern in the text: the pictures Olenin conjures in his mind are contrasted with the complicated, divergent reality he so often encounters. His infatuation with Maryanka is in this respect broadly comical. Olenin quite literally creates her, mak-ing her fit within the confines of his masculine fantasy. There is a double deception in this, for Olenin's intense interest in her physical appearance, her "strong virginal lines" (6:X/41//44), her "rising breasts outlined clearly beneath the tight cloth" and "shapely legs" (6:XXIV/92//99) betrays a plain sensuality that he is at pains to spiri-tualize, expressing an almost guilty need for justification more than any serious commitment to a romantic ideal. His curious courtship with Maryanka is shot through with these ambiguities of intent. They guarantee that mutual incomprehension which seems to take Olenin so much by surprise at the end of the novel when Maryanka barely seems to acknowledge him. What he has taken to be some sort of love turns out to have been merely a passing flirtation, an expres-sion of interest in an exotic outsider that is the unflattering mirror image of his own.

If Maryanka stubbornly fails to fit the image of feminine perfec-tion that Olenin capriciously foists upon her, an image long associ-ated with timeless divine wisdom (either as Sophia, Dante's Beatrice, or Goethe's Eternal-feminine),[17] neither do Eroshka or Lukashka fit the images of the admirable natural man that Olenin seeks to apply to them. Lukashka is supposed to be a youth of primitive, bellicose valor. To admire him, however, one must also be willing to embrace his casual brutality as evinced by his joyful murder of the Chechen scout. "Joyful" is the most appropriate adjective here. Lukashka dis-plays a delight in killing that hardly squares with romantic pieties about natural beauty and harmony. Nature is rudely (and innocently) violent. Nature's children thrill in that violence without the least compassion, despite what Rousseau would like to argue in their defense.[18] To the contrary, primitive man is perhaps too savage, and cunningly so: he is "more bestial than any beast."[19] Savagery—and the problematic character of Olenin's relation to it—are shown nowhere to better effect than at the novel's end, where Cossacks kill a group of trapped Chechens.

This is a polemical scene for anyone who should like to defend the state of nature. Cossack scouts spot a group of Chechen marauders. Lukashka heads a party of Cossacks out to meet them. He is followed by Olenin who can only observe without participating. The Cossacks find the Chechens hopelessly trapped in broad daylight, and Lukashka immediately launches an attack on them with the intent to kill all. The attack is a minor massacre; the Chechens are "hacked to pieces" (*izrublennie*) (6:XIL//145/156). Lukashka himself is wounded when he tries to save the brother of the Chechen he had killed, likely so as to profit from him at a later time. The Chechen who fired at Lukashka in turn receives a bullet in the head, an act of revenge the narrator describes with trenchant terseness: "The cornet went up to him as if intending to pass by, and with a quick movement shot him in the ear. The Chechen started up, but it was too late, and he fell" (6:XIL//145/156). Here is nature in all its majesty.

Eroshka shares many of Lukashka's qualities. He is equally brave, ruthless and feckless. He befriends Olenin not so much out of liking—how could he like such a silly creature?—but out of hope for advantage; he shows himself to be a somewhat more experienced hand than Lukashka. Olenin is guided by other assumptions, however, and he soon becomes infatuated with the old man whose vision of life is such an untroubled parody, or "innocent" perversion, of Christian belief. Eroshka merely scoffs at Olenin's uncertainty, that reflexive frailty—a tendency always to ask "Why?"—which inhibits action, and he is quite ready to enlist God in support of the casual hedonism he prefers:

"God made everything for man's pleasure. There's no sin in anything. Take a beast: a beast will live in the Tartar's reeds as well as in ours—wherever it goes, the beast's at home. Whatever God gives it, it will eat. But our priests say we'll have to lick frying pans in Hell. I think it's all a lie!"

"What's all a lie?"

"What the priests say. I'll tell you something—in Chervlenaya, the Cossack colonel himself was my blood brother. He was as fine a fellow as I was. He was killed in Chechnya. He used to say that the priests had made the whole thing up. When you croak, he used to say, grass will grow over your grave, and that will be that."

Eroshka laughed. "What a wild fellow he was!" (6:XIV//56/ 59–60)

Olenin appears to admire Eroshka's "vision" of the world. But, as with Maryanka and Lukashka, his admiration cannot be maintained because, far from being a "vision" of the world, Eroshka expresses what eludes the notion of vision as a world view or "philosophy." Why? Eroshka's view is little more than a praise of pure presentness, of being seduced by whatever takes one's fancy at a given moment, memorably captured by Oscar Wilde's jaded quip to the effect that the best way to resist temptation is to succumb to it.[20] And while this malleability of character seems to express a pure, innocent freedom, one must be very careful to define what one means by freedom in this context. For freedom is inherently ambiguous. Absolute freedom is possible strictly as a postulate: in the world, one can dispose of a relative freedom only, a freedom limited, and thus directed, by another. Eroshka expresses a freedom directed by the body, its prerogatives, and caprices. The contrary to such freedom would consist in the capacity to override the body, to deny or discipline it, associated with rationality, this being the freedom central to morality as something other than an uneasy agreement based on mutual gratification. From this latter point of view, Eroshka's freedom is mere enslavement to the mechanisms of the body, his innocence a serene amorality that views all acts gratifying the body with equanimity. Hence, if Olenin is sympathetic to the freedom that Eroshka advocates, he cannot embrace it: to do so would be to celebrate the indifference of Maryanka, the brutality of Lukashka, and the venality of Eroshka.

These characters which, as I have suggested, surround Olenin as so many different and enticing possibilities of being, do not and cannot fit the roles Olenin has assigned to them. For these are roles established by the outsider whose very ability to question and evaluate both shapes them and ensures their unsuitability. Closeness to nature, a life in immediacy, if indeed it really is so, has nothing of the romantic about it. There is not a good or bad original nature, but rather one that appears to be simply beyond ascriptions of value.

The usual argument arising from this sobering dissonance is that a stark realism triumphs in the novel over the fantastical thinking or hunger for fantasy that, one might claim, characterize Olenin's approach to the world.[21] Such arguments have a venerable pedigree— they look back to the origins of the novel in *Don Quixote*, arguably the most elaborately premeditated instance of such dissonance available in the tradition. Is this a fundamental conflict between imagination and reality? Is there any way to resolve this conflict, to avoid the need for imagination?

The Cossacks responds to this fundamental question with greatest clarity in the novel's most famous single scene, Olenin's penetration into the stag's lair in chapter XX, almost exactly midway through the narrative.[22] Many interpretations of this scene tend to see it as an ecstatic moment of reconciliation wherein Olenin experiences that "oceanic feeling," the blandly benign moment of harmony between self and other, which Romain Rolland regarded as the very essence of religious feeling, of finding oneself at home in the world.[23] It is well to note in this latter respect that Olenin's name is derived from the word for "stag" in Russian, implying that his penetration into the stag's lair is a metaphorical return home.

But the scene stands for paradox. The moment of highest individual feeling is also the moment of the most complete feeling of connectedness with all other beings. In this sense, it is not hard to understand why the scene holds the promise of reconciliation by stretching oppositions to their limits such that they meld into each other. This is not, however, a case of the extremes touching. Rather, it is a case of the dissolution of all boundaries, a reconciliation that in fact dissolves the delicate web of identities that make for conflict: it is a "moment" of nothingness brought into language by paradox. For through paradox that which is other to language, that which can only speak indirectly (thus through the imperfect device of paradox), announces itself as what limits language, and thus knowledge as well. Here the wonderful reconciliation between part and whole—also claimed to be a reconciliation of subject and object, self and other, man and nature and so on—is the opposite of what it may seem to be. What is that reconciliation? What does it mean to merge subject and object, self and other, to "perform a great feat of selflessness" as Olenin claims (6:XX//79/85)? Is it possible even to speak of this merged "entity" without effecting a betrayal, a return to the distinctions from which Olenin seeks to be liberated? Have we not in fact returned to a state prior to nature as some thing? And, if so, what exactly can this state be?

The fact is that this state cannot be any *thing*, for it entirely undermines "thinghood" or, at the very least, renders it acutely problematic. The wonderful reconciliation turns out to be a disclosure of nothingness from which Olenin must flee. By this flight Olenin signals that he cannot return to some original, pristine state. There is no state of nature, only nature, infinite and void of human traits. Natural man is just as much a negotiation with this void as his civilized counterpart. To return to our opening question, the bedrock reality of experience that the ostensibly objective narrative opposes to the imaginative projections of Olenin is also an imaginative projection, a necessary evasion of this monstrous void, with which no human being can seem to live in peace. How then does one reconcile oneself with this void?

This great question makes up a sort of Ariadne's thread by which to orient oneself within the cunning labyrinth of Tolstoy's fictional world. The enormous, hybrid creation that comes after *The Cossacks* explores this question with a complexity that had hitherto been unavailable in the novel, perhaps in any other great work of literature. For in *War and Peace* the "problem" of the void assumes its properly disproportionate proportions as the problem of the infinite, the incommensurable, the endlessly dissonant, which both demands that the imagination intervene and ensures that this intervention must fail. This combination of demand and failure presents itself as a dominant structural motif in *War and Peace* where narrative imagination wages war against the infinite, aiming at an elusive, impossible mastery.

Study 2: *War and Peace*

Mastery is the goal of war. Mastery not only over other human beings, but also, when stretched to its fullest extent, over all hindrances to human authority, foremost among which are disease and death. These separate but intimately related planes of mastery ramify through the enormous bulk of *War and Peace* in contest with a countervailing striving to relinquish striving. This contest describes a central pattern in the novel, its crucial and governing trope, formed by the interplay of the two opposing forces. For, if mastery expresses the desire for hegemony, for the complete subjection of all hostile elements in the world to the human will, relinquishment expresses a desire for reconciliation, for learning to come to terms with the world's hostile elements.

To put this contest in terms that have a broad historical resonance, one can argue that mastery is distinctively modern, a variant of the quintessentially modern striving to take control over nature—thus to fend off death and disease—rather than simply to acquiesce to the limitations it imposes on us.[24] Relinquishment as such is, then, a return to the wisdom of the ancients who considered the striving for mastery to be hubristic and potentially disastrous; for them, reconciliation with our own limitations was high, noble courage and a way of living that resolved to accept our lot as it is rather than to transform it. This is why one is well justified in referring to the striving for mastery as revolutionary, as the very essence of revolutionary zeal, for it holds within itself the profoundly revolutionary hope that nature may be brought to heel for the benefit of humanity, no matter how violent that process may be. Relinquishment is thus also a retreat from immoderate hopes in favor of a more measured and forgiving response to the conditions imposed on us by physical limitation.

To employ terms I have used above, the allegorical aspect of *War and Peace* reveals itself here at its most basic level. The allegory is again one of defeat. But this defeat brings forth ample fruit, for the entire novel is a product of that defeat, a wont of perfection, that is never satisfied, ever restless and searching. The most fascinating aspect of *War and Peace* is that the contest of opposing forces generates the immense complexity of the novel and ensures that its generative power never reaches stasis.

This view challenges assumptions common to many interpretations of the novel. The latter are revealing in their own sake, since they tend to show considerable discomfort regarding the peculiar dynamics of its structure. What I mean here is that, roughly speaking, interpretations have tended to fall either on the side of mastery or on that of relinquishment. They have not considered the possibility of interplay between the two, the Aristotelean prohibition that forces one to choose either/or instead of both/and having won the day. This hesitancy has led to accounts of the novel as either an epic, a narrative designed to encompass the whole of reality—whatever that might be—without remainder, or as an incorrigibly open, novelistic work, a sort of self-refuting *roman à thèse*, mounting a colossal attack on all attempts at mastery.

While the preceding account is of course a simplification of the novel's reception, it does give a reasonably adequate sense of how the novel has been read so as to impute to it a final position, this being a highly ironic approach for those who extol the virtues of the second tendency, relinquishment. But the novel defeats this reading, just as it defeats a reading that suggests it is comprehensive. The novel's dynamic texture permits neither mode of interpretation to prevail. Rather, each identifies an important aspect of the novel that cannot, however, claim to define a final meaning or position. Lest this determination itself seem final, I should point out that the ascription to the novel of a dynamic texture is merely a way of giving it a preliminary identity that is in fact so diversely refracted within the novel as to threaten an all too simplifying approach. While the primary opposition between mastery and relinquishment is comprehensive, it describes a dynamic movement that militates against the possibility of comprehensiveness. To impose identity such that identity itself always comes into question is perhaps the only way to approach the novel that may be sufficiently sensitive to its rhythms, that does not oversimplify or, indeed, pervert it.

To get a handle on the working of this pattern within the text, I offer what may be called a graduated approach. I shall start by considering how the constitutive opposition of the novel emerges in some of its main characters. Then, I shall provide an account of this opposition in the narrative architecture of the novel and, finally, as an abstract structure in the treatise with which it ends. At that point it shall become, I hope, a good deal more apparent that the novel struggles against approaches that would seek to fix its meaning once and for all.

Character typology

The constitutive opposition of the novel has a very obvious concrete instantiation in the two principal military commanders, Napoleon and Kutuzov. Napoleon is the epitome of the modern striving for mastery; his astounding career was taken as such by the romantic imagination, which saw in him the supreme embodiment of the striving to be a god. The novel builds on this tradition—already well established by the middle of the nineteenth century—and, in a typically Tolstoyan move, distorts it to create an utterly unromantic Napoleon.

But this is not the Napoleon whom we first encounter in the novel: that Napoleon is nothing less than an "antichrist," a mythic beast. In the opening words of Anna Pavlovna Scherer:

> Well, my prince, Genoa and Lucca are now no more than possessions, *estates*, of the Buonaparte family. No, I warn you, if you do not tell me we are at war, if you still allow yourself to palliate all the infamies, all the atrocities of that Antichrist (upon my

word, I believe it)—I no longer know you, you are no longer my
friend, you are no longer my faithful slave as you say . . . (9:I/I//1/3)

This delightful passage is much more pregnant with meaning than
one might think at first glance. For one thing, it is in French, featuring a Russian high society already vanquished by the language of the
supposed Antichrist, already open to the dangerous cultural heritage
which Napoleon embodies. For another, the term Antichrist is more
than simply jocular, it is prophetic because the Napoleonic desire to
be as a god, when taken to its logical conclusion, is a desire to achieve
a state of timeless perfection, to end time and human misery. The
conqueror rejects suffering, rejects being human and, in these
respects, the conqueror is very much the anti-Christ: the overturning
or perversion of what Christ signifies.

This beginning is indicative of the novel's profound thematic
consistency, its relentless pursuit of a problem. But it also announces
its dual aspect—to which I have already alluded—namely, that the
Napoleonic invasion, the exercise of violence on an unprecedented
scale, has both a very physical dimension, a dread immediacy, as well
as a profoundly figurative one in so far as it represents a desire to
master the very conditions of our being in the world. What is more,
the conqueror's lust suggests that the latter is wholly dependent
on the former: that it is the despairing, fearful call of the body that
fuels the desire to overcome our mortal estate, to be like a god. Hence,
this desire is immersed in irony, since it can only issue from a creature
having nothing in common with a god.

Irony defines Napoleon's role in the novel. The first description of
the great man in action occurs during the narrative of the battle of
Austerlitz, one of the novel's decisive battle scenes. The narrator
provides a striking picture of Napoleon observing his troops from a
high point as they go into battle against their confused, dispirited
counterparts who are stuck in low ground, engulfed by a sea of
fog: ". . . Napoleon stood, surrounded by his marshals, it was perfectly light. Over him was the clear blue sky, and the enormous ball
of the sun, like an enormous, hollow, crimson float, bobbed on the
surface of the milky sea of fog" (9:I/3/XIV//333/272). Not only does
Napoleon stand above the battle, like a god, he is also on the same
level with the sun. These physical details easily pass over into a figuration of Napoleon as a divine man, inheritor of the ancient hubris of
Alexander and Caesar, as well as the modern arrogance of Louis XIV,

"*le roi soleil.*" But this description, presented by an ostensibly objective, "classical" narrator, runs aground ambiguously after the battle, when Napoleon appears again, this time filtered through the ecstatic consciousness of the badly wounded Prince Andrei Bolkonsky. This Napoleon gloats over his victory. In a rather macabre way, he surveys the dead and wounded with what appears to be a feeling of smug superiority that reveals the ugly, petty human hiding behind the grandeur of the conqueror.

This presentation of Napoleon gains in authority as the novel progresses, since the main narrator also takes it up, in a typical example of the fugue-like quality of the narrative.[25] The main narrator only does so, however, after Napoleon has entered Russia. And, even by this stage of the novel, ambiguity cannot be totally excluded. For example, there is a very famous suite of scenes in Part 1 of Book III that depicts Napoleon in his two aspects, god-like and pathetically human, at the very beginning of the invasion. His unperturbed attitude to the Polish Uhlans who drown themselves in the Niemen river directly in front of him shows the icy lack of compassion characteristic of a god, whereas the twitching, self-absorbed, self-justifying creature that greets Balashev is deeply and miserably human, a comic buffoon.

The latter picture starts to take over with defeat, and this is arguably as it should be given that defeat is not divine but human. After Borodino, Napoleon appears almost always as the comic buffoon. All grandeur which may have originally attached to him dissipates before the tiny, vain and disgusting human being. The great work of the conqueror, hiding one's wretched, finite humanity, fails and is bound to fail. That is the "lesson" of Napoleon: he first appears as a tragic figure, attempting to encroach on the precincts of the gods, and leaves the stage of the novel as a farcical one.

Kutuzov is far less turbulent. An almost preternatural calm constitutes the primary source of his peculiar charm and power. Kutuzov appears somewhat earlier in the novel than Napoleon, in one of its more amusing episodes, the inspection of troops at Braunau with which Part 2 of Book II begins. It is fitting that Kutuzov should first appear in this light because he is a comic character wholly different from Napoleon. Kutuzov does not seek to hide human frailty—there is thus no acidulous revelation regarding him as there is in the case of Napoleon—and the fact that he orders the troops to change out of their dress uniforms into their rough marching ones is a characteristic twist. Rather than parade his infallibility, Kutuzov seeks quite the opposite, with cunning and care for his troops. The irony here is that Kutuzov has the troops hide their genuine competence in furtherance of a sly stratagem. If one takes this play further, one might argue that Kutuzov's flawed, human *bonhomie* is little more than a ruse intended to deceive the more powerful and aggressive.[26]

If Napoleon seeks vainly to rule, then, Kutuzov adapts himself to an infinite nexus of changing conditions. He refuses to act with Napoleon's reckless arrogance because he knows better. What he knows better is that we know and can know very little, that our cognitive task is to remain open to the flow of events, to perceive the finest differentiations or changes, and never to be so foolish as to think that we can shape events, thus imposing our will on the world.

Kutuzov's relinquishment of mastery is not, then, some sort of "wise passivity" or resignation before the impossibility of controlling events, but an active "hearing," a directing of one's attention "outward." Kutuzov's complex attitude is described well by Prince Andrei on the eve of Borodino, the most important of all battles in the novel:

> How and why it happened, Prince Andrei could in no way have explained, but after this meeting with Kutuzov, he went back to his regiment relieved with regard to the general course of things and with regard to the man to whom it had been entrusted. The more he saw the absence of anything personal in this old man, in whom there seemed to remain only the habit of passions, and, instead of intelligence (which groups events and draws conclusions), only the ability to calmly contemplate the course of events, the more calmed he felt over everything being as it had to be. "He won't have anything of his own. He won't invent, won't undertake anything," thought Prince Andrei, "but he'll listen to everything, remember everything, put everything in its place, won't hinder anything useful or allow anything harmful. He understands that there is something stronger and more significant than his will— the inevitable course of events—and he's able to see them, able to understand their significance, and, in view of that significance, is able to renounce participating in those events, renounce his personal will and direct it elsewhere . . ." (11:III/2/XVI//174/744–5)

Disinterest and contemplation are the two key ways of describing Kutuzov's attitude. Disinterest is a very loaded term associated with a god-like capacity to perceive totality, and not run astray in the particular based on demanding personal interest. Since this term introduces a crucial layer of thought in *War and Peace*, I should like to dwell a little on the distinction between disinterest and interest from a more abstract viewpoint before returning to Kutuzov's role in the novel.

Interest describes a being among things (*inter-esse*)[27] whereby things are always making claims on us, drawing us to them as potentially satisfying physical need or desire. As such, interest expresses both the inherent immediacy and selfishness of desire, both that a claim is being made on me and that I must act to address that claim. One can argue hence that all action is interested, that there is simply no kind of action that would not be interested. Disinterest and inaction are therefore to some degree synonymous or equivalent. That is why there is almost always a distinction between the life of action (*vita activa*) and the life of contemplation (*vita contemplativa*), the former being a life of interest, of active involvement in the practical task of satisfaction that is the life of the body, the latter a life of disinterest, of contemplative detachment from the practical task of living and the traumatic cares of the body. This latter kind of life has long been associated with relinquishment of the world, the retreat into monastic quietude, and it is one of the more intriguing, indeed "orientalizing," aspects of *War and Peace* that one finds almost the reverse: that the life of relinquishment is in its own sense an active one, a life very much in the world, not one withdrawn from it.[28]

Prince Andrei's observations concerning Kutuzov make the case for this view. Kutuzov is at the center of action. He appears to be directing it according to a grand strategy or plan. But this is manifestly not the case. His activity is more akin to interpretation or divination, of reading from the whole of a given circumstance what is and will be, rather than succumbing to the temptation to make it submit to his will as Napoleon does. Kutuzov is the bedrock antipode to Napoleon and the modernity that Napoleon expresses in an extreme way: Kutuzov tries to see the whole from outside the limitations imposed by his physical place within it, whereas Napoleon cannot see it otherwise.[29] Moreover, Kutuzov's opposition to Napoleon is also explicitly associated with an opposition between arrogant Western modernity and Russian humility and good sense. For, as the narrator notes, a Russian "does not believe it possible to know anything fully" (11:III/1/X//48/639). A genuine Russian lives intuitively, rooted in his native soil and traditions, and thus the Russian has no need to seek out new experiences and lands; rootless Western modernity is inherently aggressive and eager to inflict violence on others to disguise its own rootlessness. Russians have only to turn back to themselves to find the best way of overcoming the ills of the West, its profanity, and lust for blood.

One of the novel's most famous characters, Platon Karataev (about whom more below), is the embodiment of this point of view. He also reveals an extraordinary aspect of the novel's characters: that almost none is neutral, that many can be aligned with either the Napoleonic or Kutuzovian tendency in the novel as if these were great structural magnetic forces. While Platon Karataev stands with Kutuzov, as do characters as diverse as Tushin and, indeed, Natasha Rostova, a line of characters, like Dolokhov and Speransky stand with Napoleon. The latter identification is particularly clear since the narrative associates them with Napoleon by means of similar physical or emotional traits, like white hands in the case of Speransky, or affection for one's poor mother in the case of Dolokhov.

Unique among these characters, however, are the two main heroes of the novel, Prince Andrei and Pierre Bezukhov. They are unique because they bring the conflict between the Napoleonic and Kutuzovian poles to the level of an internal contest and thereby define tragic and comic elements in each pole in terms of a conscious struggle to grasp truth and to forge a durable identity in light of that truth. Prince Andrei and Pierre thus give voice to the novel's underlying dynamic not in the traditional sense of an exteriorized battle between different communities and the different ways of being expressed by those communities, but in the form of a largely internal struggle that has more to do with combating one's community than with conforming to it.

Prince Andrei Bolkonsky

Prince Andrei is clearly with Napoleon at the beginning of the novel. His subsequent trajectory is one of defeated hopes, his early admiration for Napoleon having been dashed by the combined influence of Kutuzov and Austerlitz. This admiration reveals Prince Andrei's essentially tragic stance: he cannot accept the world as it is with its brutal and messy contingency. He seeks plan and order but finds neither. Instead he finds the infinite in the formless form of that "lofty, infinite sky with clouds racing across it," which he discovers while lying prostrate on the battlefield of Austerlitz:

> Though five minutes earlier Prince Andrei had been able to say a few words to the soldiers transporting him, now, with his eyes fixed directly on Napoleon, he was silent . . . To him at that moment all the interests that occupied Napoleon seemed so insignificant, his hero himself seemed so petty to him, with his petty vanity and joy in victory, compared with that lofty, just, and kindly sky, which he had seen and understood, that he was unable to answer him.
>
> Then, too, everything seemed so useless and insignificant compared with that stern and majestic way of thinking called up in him by weakness from loss of blood, suffering great pain, and the expectation of imminent death. Looking into Napoleon's eyes, Prince Andrei thought about the insignificance of grandeur, about the insignificance of life, the meaning of which no one could understand, and about the still greater insignificance of death, the meaning of which no one among the living could understand or explain. (9:I/3/XIX//358–9/292–3)

What does Prince Andrei garner from this? That "Nothing, nothing is certain, except the insignificance of everything that I can comprehend, and the grandeur of something incomprehensible but most important!" (9:I/3/XIX//359/293).

This vision of the infinite compels Prince Andrei to retreat. After returning to Russia and the death of his wife, he hides in the almost sepulchral world of Bogucharovo. If his vision of the infinite is providential, it is also crushing. Prince Andrei's subsequent trajectory in the novel reflects unease about his discovery at Austerlitz; he is capable neither of fully embracing nor rejecting this discovery and remains entrapped within a continuous, exhausting pattern of oscillation between the two possibilities. If he seeks to hide from the world at Bogucharovo, he soon tires of this quiescent state. The need to act is too strong. Soon he discovers Natasha and his interest in the world returns. At first he leaves Bogucharovo for St Petersburg and falls under the spell of another avatar of Napoleon, Speransky, but his love for Natasha trumps his love for politics (at least momentarily) and he grows disillusioned with Speransky. His love for Natasha also fails, however; he offers himself up for death at Borodino as one who despairs of satisfaction in this world.

Lest this sound too melodramatic, too much like a nineteenth-century art of the soap opera, it is well to note that Prince Andrei's oscillation reflects a powerfully tragic sense of human possibility. Prince Andrei is not able to achieve satisfaction. His only satisfaction can come from mastery—a complete mastery—and, despite the revelation of the infinite at Austerlitz, he is never capable of coming to terms with the impossibility of mastery. If the world is infinite, thus always out of reach of human definition, any claim to mastery, cognitive or other, cannot meet with success. Prince Andrei is condemned to repetition. The problem here is more complicated than it may seem. For, if action is predicated on its efficaciousness, thus on the capacity of action to achieve the ends to which it strives, the impotence with which the infinite confronts us puts all human action in question. How is that so?

If the world is infinite, any definition is as good (and bad) as any other, any way of constructing the world is in the final account a falsification because there always must be some remainder, which simply cannot be resolved within the cognitive network (other than as something which cannot be so resolved, that is, as a limitless limit). In the infinite there is always more. This entails that there can be simply no way of assuring that what we know is indeed what we know. For the remainder that exceeds our cognitive network is crucial, casting all we know into a different, perpetually unsure light. It is this tendency which leads to major shifts in perceptions of the world and has been referred to as a "paradigm shift" in the context of such changes in scientific understanding. While this remainder may serve only to emphasize the tenuous, provisional character of the reality we accept, it is quite enough to justify far broader suspicions, for it makes little sense to claim that one can know a part of the infinite, some core whose stability is not always already undermined: to know a part of the infinite is little more than a sarcasm. Hence, if I may hesitate before jumping in front of a car to prove my agnosticism, there are many other kinds of action whose basis in reality is more obviously insecure. If, for example, I scrupulously manage my health, that grand army of processes that take place in my body and in its interaction with the environment, will I live longer, and better? These regimes of action require a greater leap of faith because their complexity indicates clearly that there is no way of obtaining definitive cognitive assurance that they will achieve the desired result. This latter fact, that reality remains forever recalcitrant, that I am not capable of assuring definitively that any of my actions will achieve the goals I set for them, returns us to our incorrigible frailty. For the future is both enticing, the home of the new and unexpected in a hopeful sense, and menacing, the home of the completely expected, death, along with the unexpected in its most ominous, despairing sense, that of the catastrophic, deadly event.

Prince Andrei expresses a desire to live with the freedom of the former—the openness of the infinite—but his greater, more durable desire is to avoid the latter, the abject insecurity of life. This latter desire is a tragic aspiration because it seeks emancipation from the tightening noose of death and, in so doing, must reject life along with it as the realm of death: that to be born is to be born to die prevails in tragic thought. Put in other terms, Prince Andrei's faith in death overcomes his faith in life, as his behavior at Borodino amply demonstrates. On the eve of Borodino Prince Andrei confesses to Pierre that he knows too much (perhaps that he finally accepts what he has known all along): " 'Ah my friend, lately it's become hard for me to live. I see that I've begun to understand too much. And it's not good for man to taste of the tree of knowledge of good and evil' " (11: III/2/XXV//211/776). This statement seems to reflect a startling dreamlike vision he had only a short time before his meeting with Pierre. This vision depicts an ascent from the human to a position that is outside the human, one akin to death:

> And from the height of that picture, all that used to torment and preoccupy him was suddenly lit up by a cold, white light, without shadows, without perspective, without clear-cut outlines. The whole of life presented itself to him as a magic-lantern into which he had long been looking through a glass and in artificial light. Now he suddenly saw these badly daubed pictures without a glass, in bright daylight. "Yes, yes, there they are, those false images that excited, delighted and tormented me," he said to himself, turning over in his imagination the main pictures of his magic lantern of life, looking at them now in that cold, white daylight— the clear notion of death. (11:III/2/XXIV//203/769)

Prince Andrei does not, however, die at Borodino despite the awful wound he receives, as if on purpose. (Why did he not flinch with the shell whirling immediately in front of him?) Yet, even though Prince Andrei's "story-line" continues, enough to restore Natasha to life, he is dead in the more profound sense that he has indeed accepted the paramountcy of death, and that acceptance first comes to light at Borodino.

Pierre Bezukhov

Pierre has a more subtle case of Prince Andrei's illness. For the sake of a certain explanatory symmetry, I should like to consider Pierre a comic character in contrast to Prince Andrei. While this is not wholly inaccurate, it is ultimately misleading, and I shall suggest why at the appropriate point. Like Prince Andrei, Pierre is beset by crises. Yet, he spends a good portion of the first half of the novel in a state of relative equilibrium as he rather comically shows how passivity can be everything but wise. If Prince Andrei actively pursues the Napoleonic legacy, Pierre is all too susceptible to influence: he seems to be—at least initially—something of a man without qualities, and others are all too eager to fill in the empty canvas to their own advantage. This is manifestly the case with both of Pierre's early guides, Anna Mikhailovna Drubetskaia and Prince Vassily Kuragin, the former seeking funds and influence for her son, Boris, the latter for himself and his sons who, as he makes clear to Anna Pavlovna Scherer, cost him quite a lot.

The typically Tolstoyan irony here is that Pierre's passivity leads to fantastic worldly success, immense wealth, and acquisition of a beautiful wife, Princess Hélène. This is precisely the kind of success to which the cunning man of action, the Napoleonic or Dolokhovian rake, would seem to aspire in the social world, that constant combat for status and favor which has its own generals, master planners, and foot soldiers. One of the signal events that defines this irony is the notorious duel with Dolokhov. (That this duel is a miniature of the greater contest between Napoleon and Kutuzov has been the subject of some comment.[30]) Yet Pierre's unexpected success leads to a profound crisis in his life analogous to that which Prince Andrei experiences after the battle of Austerlitz.

In the contrapuntal pattern characteristic of their relationship in the novel, Prince Andrei's retreat after Austerlitz is in sharp contrast to the result of Pierre's crisis after the duel, a new, floridly humble, activism under the guidance of the Freemason, Bazdeyev. Yet, as Pierre begins to take a more active role in his life, convinced by those around him that he has the power to do so, he meets with repeated failures, a circumstance that matches Prince Andrei's experience.

Among these failures the most decisive and strange is his desire to save Russia by killing Napoleon. Pierre first expresses this desire in a comical chapter of Book III where his strained manipulation of the number 666 leads him to arrive at the conclusion that he, *l'russe Besuhof*, is destined to kill Napoleon. This chapter has garnered much attention because it so wickedly lampoons the pretensions of planners, of military strategists, political reformers, indeed, of all those whose very existence depends on the assumption that there is a human capacity to shape and direct events.

Pierre's execution of the plan is exemplary of the contrast between him and Prince Andrei. Pierre is easily sidetracked: he simply does not have the single-minded determination of Prince Andrei. This is evident from the very beginning of the novel when Pierre breaks a promise not to indulge in further debauches with Dolokhov and Anatol Kuragin. Pierre is too easily prey to the world—too much swayed by its everyday demands on him—and, in this sense, he shows to what degree he is unsuited to pursue the kind of mastery that absorbs Prince Andrei's life. Characteristic of Pierre's attachment to the world is that he ends up saving a baby girl in the embers of burning Moscow while on his quest to kill the French emperor. And, instead of achieving his objective, as the "chosen" *l'russe Besuhof*, he ends up a prisoner of the French.

Pierre's captivity is harrowing. He is saved by chance—by his face-to-face meeting with Davout—and witnesses an execution thereafter, an event that forces him to confront the question of human capacity and freedom to shape events. He asks: Why do these young men kill? What drives them to it? And he simply cannot find any answers for such questions. At this point, the lowest ebb of Pierre's life, he meets the crucial figure who will transform him, at least for a short while—for no transformation holds for long in the novel. This figure is Platon Karataev, a complexly simple and idiosyncratic avatar of Kutuzov, a necessarily enigmatic embodiment of active passivity who could be at home as easily in a Christian as in a Buddhist framework.

Karataev teaches nothing, no doctrine, no way of life; rather, he simply is, a self-refuting sign of pure being. Acting effortlessly in fluid harmony with his surrounding world, he singles nothing out, covets nothing, and shows no traces of reflective thought. Karataev is complete, free of interest, the seduction of the particular. the metaphor attached to him is that of sphericality, a metaphor traditionally associated with completeness. Pierre tries hard to emulate this peculiar creature who lives the sort of reconciliation described in *The Cossacks*. But Pierre's attachment to the world prevails; his marriage to Natasha is a fatal corruption of Karataev's "teaching." At the end of the First Epilogue to the novel, Pierre has effectively turned away from Karataev, too much drawn to the world to truly emulate him, too interested to achieve the sort of disinterest that defines Karataev's divine purity and freedom.

***

Is Pierre really all that different from Prince Andrei? For, by the end of the First Epilogue to *War and Peace*, it seems that Pierre is bound to turn away from relinquishment, the wise renunciation of mastery so positively marked in the novel. While there is some difference between the two heroes, it is less, however, than one might think. The distinction between tragic and comic that I have introduced is helpful in this respect, as well as in identifying the central philosophical issues involved.

As terms, both tragic and comic define attitudes to our interestedness in the world, to the fact that, as noted above, we are always drawn into things: in a word, we are creatures of desire. But tragic and comic forms of desire differ greatly, and they inaugurate correspondingly different narrative patterns. Tragic desire seeks completion, an ironical self-cancellation in the apotheosis of final satisfaction. As in Goethe's *Faust*, the temptation to completion reveals itself either in the striving for absolute knowledge, the sort of immediate intuition of totality associated with God, or erotic oblivion, an immersion in pure, dissolutive animality. Prince Andrei exemplifies the former, and Anna Karenina the latter, tendency, as we shall see. In both cases, desire seeks to eliminate itself, to achieve a freedom from unending repetition. Comic desire rejects this stark and self-immolating singularity of purpose, delighting in the very conditions the tragic cannot tolerate: in the circularity of its own perpetuation, its constant self-renewal, that continual turning back in moving forward that is the texture of time comic desire weaves. The comic is the refusal of finality the tragic so forcefully seeks to achieve. Whereas the tragic resolves to conclude the negotiation between mind and body that has been, through many inflections, the central generative tension in our tradition (as we saw with the *Phaedrus*), the comic resolves not to conclude the negotiation, but rather to frustrate it.

From this perspective, Prince Andrei and Pierre are ultimately not different in terms of their supreme objective, which is the same as Olenin's—to achieve a final reconciliation with the world, to be at home in it. Moreover, neither is capable of achieving that end: Kutuzovian disinterest cannot take hold of their lives in a sustained manner. This incapacity leads Prince Andrei to a rejection of the world as ridiculous farce; in Pierre, to the contrary, it leads to continued, but precarious (and likely ill-fated) engagement.[31]

Anomalies of structure

The structural anomalies attributed to *War and Peace* have much to do with this contest between contrasting attitudes to the world, between tragic and comic energies, between the striving for mastery identified with Prince Andrei and the relinquishment of striving identified with Pierre. To get a sense of these structural anomalies in their proper context, I should like to give a further account of how the novel has been received. The critical reception tells a tale of confusion and bewilderment regarding the form of the novel, one suggesting that Tolstoy's claim for the generic waywardness of *War and Peace* was by no means unjustified.[32]

When *War and Peace* first came out serially in the mid-1860s, critics complained about its formlessness, that there seemed to be no plot, no particular direction in the structure of the action (although, of course, the general direction was quite well-known). This claim for the novel's lack of form, initially a claim either of perplexity or indictment, was transformed much later into a claim for a specific strategy; no longer was formlessness simply reflective of clumsiness on the part of the author, but became instead a sign of his agility, either as an unparalleled analyst of "reality"—whatever that might be—or as a destroyer of the myths of narrative, of those elaborately false (because partial) accounts of this "reality" that seek to make the partial, relative or near-sighted into an absolute vision. But there is also a countertradition in the critical reception of the novel which has noticed that the initial impression of formlessness is deceiving and based on an exceedingly limited notion of what constitutes form. This arm of the critical reception has identified the immense network of connections in the novel, the repetitions of phrases, situations, and patterns of action, and has concluded that the novel is a cunningly structured whole, a triumph of ingenious and innovative form.[33]

The underlying question here is one of unity: Is the novel a unity or not? Those critics who argue at some level that the novel is formless or aims to reveal the weaknesses of form claim that it does not possess unity or that it possesses a "negative unity," that of its strategy to undermine unity. Those critics who argue that the novel is formally complex and incisive make an opposing claim for a positive unity. This disagreement has to do with an underlying agreement as to what unity means.[34] That is where the problem begins. For the primary formal innovation of *War and Peace* lies in its creation of a dynamic unity whose attempt to encompass the infinite reflects at once both critical perspectives without succumbing to either.

The basic problem the narrative sets for itself is announced in Book III, roughly halfway through the novel and at a key juncture where the tide begins to turn in favor of the hitherto beleaguered Russian army. The narrator claims that the chief problem of historical writing has been its inability to write events as a whole, to grasp them in their continuity and full complexity, which involves an infinite chain of causes. According to the narrator, historians have accorded greater authority to specific causal chains, carving them out of the infinite causal nexus of historical continuity without any justification other than an obliging fiction, that of the "great man" or god-like historical figure. Historians have assumed an essentially Napoleonic stance toward the writing of history with a rather optimistic or arrogant conception of human causal efficacy. But, the narrator argues, if the causes are indeed infinite, then the historians can only have written lies.

The narrator opposes to this a different, holistic conception of writing that adopts the innovations of calculus as its model. This writing aims to express the laws governing those patterns that emerge in the continuous process of history, thereby assimilating human action to natural processes. For the stratagem of modern mathematics reflected in calculus, the revolutionary innovation in regard to the infinite, is not to enumerate fixed points, obviously an impossible task (at least for the finite mind), but to describe patterns of relative change in continuous processes.[35] The narrative structure of *War and Peace* reflects this relational conception of writing, if only imperfectly, featuring complex repetitions of narrative trajectories, situations, and events, all of which may be understood as identifying dynamic patterns in history. Formal similarity may thus permit construction of a typology of such patterns in the novel, thereby inviting the inference that all human action can be "mapped" so as to offer the means to create an overarching structure, a unified metahistory of humanity not dissimilar to myth.

The first book of the novel provides a broad example of the comparative technique essential to this metahistorical task, setting three groups against each other in three different locations, St Petersburg, Moscow, and the countryside as represented by Bald Hills. Prince Vassily's family is representative of St Petersburg society, the Rostov family plays the same role for Moscow as does the family of Prince Bolkonsky for the countryside. Here location and social unit provide bases for comparison. So does the action. For each sequence of scenes illustrates a variant of a singular pattern of action, proceeding from a certain order to the collapse or transformation of that order into its opposite. This pattern emerges in the opening sequence with the inanity of Prince Ippolite Kuragin's "joke," a collapse into nonsense that defines and saves the soirée, as well as with the riotous debauch that ends the evening for Pierre. The lively world of the Rostovs' collapses into the dirge of Count Bezukhov's death; Prince Andrei's return to Bald Hills ends in a transformative departure.

This technique also has the effect of producing a novel that reads as if everything were taking place in the present—as if the novel were simply conveying what is in its full presence in the here and now—but in which repetitions and similarities begin to accumulate, affirming at once the temporality of events and the atemporal patterns which they continually repeat. What I mean here is that temporality emerges as syntax, as a kind of bare order or initial condition of knowing, from which pure, abstract structures, of collapse, quest, despair, and so on develop. The novel is thus in continual motion, moving from preoccupation with the immediate to the apprehension of structures that belie the immediate because they show how situated it is within an abstract paradigm of action. There is literally nothing new under the sun. Rather, all events express themselves only within an underlying pattern and are thus a continual return of that pattern. Linear temporality, the flow of action to an end, is simply another return in a vast system governed by patterns that reveals basic laws of action.

This temporal signature in the novel reflects the contrast between mastery and relinquishment in the following manner. Relinquishment tends toward pure presentness, an immediate immersion in the flow of events. Mastery seeks to interrupt that flow with a view to shaping it, to reducing it to certain structure. And just as the novel features a contest between these opposing tendencies in its two main characters, its structure features a similar contest between the openness of the narrative experience and the closure of the patterning which gives that experience coherence. The novel both stresses immediacy and the means by which that immediacy becomes coherent as such: there is in this sense a careful interplay at work, one that all novels possess to some degree, but not necessarily with comparable equanimity.

This interplay may be best examined from the point of view of genre. In his brilliantly concise essay, "From Allegories to Novels," the Argentine writer Jorge Luis Borges identifies the novel as "a fable of individuals" in contrast to the allegory, which is a "fable of abstractions."[36] What is the operative contrast here? Allegory stands for that mode of thinking which wrests from temporal experience an underlying structure or pattern, suggesting that a given configuration of action has greater universal significance. A fine example of this is the quest narrative of *The Cossacks*, which is not merely the description of a trip to the Caucasus, but of a quest for freedom or lost immediacy. Now it is hard to imagine any kind of literature that can avoid allegory so defined; and, indeed, allegory in this broadened sense describes any procedure by which a certain narrative is transformed from a mere enumeration of "happenings" to the expression of a certain continuous event, of a certain way of imposing meaning on the bare bones of actions or events that wrests them from their mute particularity.

Borges points out that the novel is the genre that most seeks to evade the allegorizing impulse, achieving thus the illusion of portraying what is in its particularity. This aspect of the novel remains its essential "trick" or *coup de main*, the origin of its claim to realism, and its fertility as a democratic genre, one that takes all things as particular individuals without exclusion and, to that extent, makes them equal. Hierarchy resides in allegory not in the novel's predilection for the particular. Borges also points out, however, that allegory is not so easy to discard. For one thing, language is inherently generalizing. Nothing can be referred to in itself, a general term is always required, and that general term cannot penetrate the particular as it is in its particularity: a word always *re*-presents. Moreover, a word is part of a greater conceptual scheme that generalizes, abstracts and, in so doing, makes decisions as to what can and cannot be included: hierarchy is unavoidable, especially as the representative aspect of language is stretched further, as it is in any text. Hence, the novel's tendency toward the individual particular is the triumph of a certain strategy of allegorizing or representing the world, a strategy that artfully commits to self-concealment, even (and, perhaps, especially) when the novel seems most transparently to reveal its own workings as a way of exposing its artificiality.

This tension between allegory and novel is usefully descriptive of the tension between patterning and immediacy in *War and Peace*, the closure of a grand metanarrative of epic scale and the novelistic openness of the diverse events that are its "objects." For *War and Peace* is not a novel in the Borgesian sense, nor is it a one-sided unity in the sense relevant to the critical tradition. To the contrary, it is a dynamic work that tries to reconcile allegorical generality with the novel's respect for grasping particularity, a reality supposedly "as it is." *War and Peace* thus creates a more profound, complex unity by describing the dynamic interplay between these opposing emphases, neither of which may be grasped in isolation from the other, whether they be whole and part, collectivity and individual, or object and subject.

The philosophy of history
The magnificently strange, and frequently maligned, essay with which the novel ends provides an interesting conceptualization of the novel's decisive structure and convincing reasons for why reconciliation is impossible. This essay serves as the capstone to the numerous asides and narrative speculations on history that begin with the first chapter of Book III. All the speculations are concerned with the fundamental issue of human agency, whether human action can determine history, the flow of events, or whether the reverse is the case: that human beings are borne along the current of events without any power to influence them. As a more abstract question, the issue of human agency in the novel usually coalesces into a discussion of the fundamental problem of freedom, of whether human beings are free to do as they see fit or trapped in an ironclad causal chain that our incorrigible ignorance hides from us. From the point of view of many characters, a necessarily limited one, events seem to be governed by an ever elusive contingency. The narrator suggests, however, that contingency results from a purely human perspective and is not part of reality "in itself."

There is significant equivocation in the novel regarding the status of reality as it is "in itself." While the narrator suggests in places that nothing happens outside God's will, that there is indeed an overall order to reality, he rarely makes this declaration explicitly. Yet, the entire argument against historical writing supports the assumption of order, even if it is hidden. For this argument is not purely negative; it does not simply debunk historians' inadequate understanding of the complexity involved in writing history. Rather, the various arguments advanced in favor of calculus or a law-based approach to historical events, to the making of narratives that address faults in their predecessors, suggest that there are laws of nature that apply equally well to human beings. Despite this suggestion, cognitive limitation assures us that a full and final narrative cannot be achieved.

Whence this cognitive limitation? After all, if laws of history can be discovered, why would it then be impossible to know history from any particular instantiation of those laws? Why does the part not reveal the whole? There must be some form of slippage that undermines the harmony of part and whole which the discovery of laws is supposed to bring about. In the final chapters of the Second Part of the Epilogue, the narrator offers an explanation for this slippage by means of an essentially anthropological argument. The narrator argues that all cognition emerges from a peculiarly asymmetrical relation, that between reason and consciousness. The narrator's concise summary is worth quoting:

> Reason expresses the laws of necessity. Consciousness expresses the essence of freedom.
>
> Freedom, not limited by anything, is the essence of life in the consciousness of man. Necessity without content is man's reason with its three forms.
>
> Free will is that which is examined. Necessity is that which examines. Freedom is content. Necessity is form.
>
> Only by separation of the two sources of cognition, which are related to each other as form to content, do we get the distinct, mutually exclusive, and unfathomable concepts of freedom and necessity.
>
> Only by their union do we get a clear picture of the life of man.
>
> Outside these two concepts, mutually defining in their union as form and content, no picture of life is possible. (12:2E/X//336/1210)

This definition assumes "a" plenitude, consciousness, that by its very nature cannot be grasped by reason. Reason functions to carve up or count that plenitude, which, strictly speaking, cannot be anything other than the other of any and all things. It follows that the plenitude as it is in itself must remain elusively, absolutely infinite, out of reach of defining reason, and can be grasped only as a logical postulate or inference—the "stuff" from which reason constructs a world and which, as its condition of possibility, must subtract itself from that construction.

A thorny question remains: What is this "stuff," this plenitude? How can it have an "is" if it cannot be defined or known as some thing? The narrator indicates that it is only through consciousness that we know we are alive: ". . . consciousness is a totally separate source of self-knowledge, independent of reason. Through reason man observes himself, but he knows himself only through consciousness." The narrator then affirms that: "Without consciousness of oneself, no observation and no application of reason are thinkable" (12:2E/VIII//323/1201). Hence, the crucial foundation of life, being itself, cannot be brought under the control of reason but must necessarily evade it: what seems nearest is farthest away.

If one were to stop here, it would seem that any rational account must fail, must betray what it attempts to convey. Every rational account leaves a remainder, some "hard" kernel of reality that resists and remains concealed. No matter what approach one might take, even a mathematically-modeled reconciliation of part and whole, one can never return to the seamless purity of that "stuff," that plenitude of consciousness, from which all things emerge. If that is so, it seems problematic—to say the least—to claim that a mathematical approach to narrative may be superior to the traditional causal approach. For, if reason cannot grasp the whole in itself, how can it be said to grasp anything other than necessary illusions, perhaps renewed for modern tastes, but still constituting shadows on the wall of a cave-like enclosure?

This is a very complex aspect of *War and Peace*: a fascinating combination of rationality and irrationality courses through the entire text, which is at once an attempt to create a paradigmatic narrative and a declaration of the impossibility of doing so. If the great shapes of action may be inventoried, the reasons behind those actions, the why and wherefore of their coming as and when they do, remain utterly in darkness. The laws of history may give us a neat taxonomy of historical possibility, but they can do next to nothing in regard to what animates those actions; and, in this respect, one is struck throughout the novel by the sheer ineffability of action. The deepest recesses of what is, the realm of what the narrator refers to as consciousness, can never be grasped, much less exhausted, and all that can be done is to attain a certain formal facility that can never achieve the goal of knowledge. Reconciliation, harmony with the world, an end to action, and the suffering that generates it, are nowhere to be found. We are driven along by forces we cannot understand, forces concerning which we can do little more than construct palliative or useful fictions. We are the creature compelled to create.[37]

Study 3: *Anna Karenina*

The theme of reconciliation haunts *Anna Karenina*. The famous opening aphorism, "All happy families are alike; each unhappy family is unhappy in its own way," sets the stage for a somber narrative of dissimulation, where action in all its variety follows from discord and the ever present desire to flee the source of discord, that fundamental absence of plenitude which distinguishes us as human beings. For happiness, contentment or satisfaction, is plenitude, in its immaculate placidity, nothing occurs or can occur. But unhappiness does not arise from plenitude but from its absence: if happy families are static, statuesque, and stable in the dreadful sense of a complete equilibrium—a night in which all cows are black—unhappy families are uneasy, restless, and ever active. This is so precisely because unhappy families are lacking. The absence they experience absorbs their life, which is nothing more than a striving to overcome that absence.

Like few other novels, *Anna Karenina* lays bare the frailty of our state, the ubiquity of absence and the latter's supreme role in shaping our attitude toward the world. All action longs to turn away from or overcome absence, but in doing so remains implacably conditioned by it. This fatal pattern courses through the entire novel, distinguishing the latter from *War and Peace* both in the more sharply closed quality of the narrative, where all events appear to lead to a catastrophic end, and in the symbolic armature that supports it, which is arguably more portentous.

Let me explain what I mean a little more carefully. Whereas *War and Peace* begins *in medias res* thereby maximally expressing the openness of the narrative as a narrative in the present, *Anna Karenina* begins with two statements that impose an ambiguous contour on the action, placing it within a completed narrative whole. These two statements are the famous epigraph and the opening aphorism. The epigraph, "Vengeance is mine; I will repay," has occasioned a great deal of comment due to its somewhat complicated provenance in both the Old and New Testaments.[38] Notwithstanding this provenance, the plain predictive force of the epigraph is clear: vengeance will be enacted. Even if the particulars of that vengeance are not immediately clear, the line of action—one that cannot but lead to an unpleasant or catastrophic end—is. Moreover, the opening aphorism also imposes a contour on the narrative, suggesting that it concerns, and, indeed, can only concern, the kind of distressed striving I noted above, an impression heightened by the succeeding paragraph that leads into a carefully structured description of the absence of structure in the Oblonsky household where, we are told, "All was confusion." Taken together, the epigraph and opening aphorism not only suggest the limits of the narrative, but its thoroughly mediated nature, that it is very much a particular telling of a particular story.

There is another aspect to this opening that confirms its mediated nature: the careful ordering of layers of authority. The first voice we encounter, God's, is at once outside the novel as an epigraph, but inside of it to the degree the epigraph imposes itself on the narrative. The epigraph can be said to contain the novel just as God contains the lives of those created by and thus absolutely subject to Him. The opening aphorism presents, presumably, the voice of the implied author of the text whose role is only superficially similar to God's. For the aphorism attempts to conceal its contingent origins by its sheer absoluteness, by means of the universal quantifier, "all." Since human voices are stuck in time and space, thus relative and contingent, the absolute pretensions of the aphorism are no more than pretension and, in a deeper sense, whose significance I will address below, deception.[39] What is more, the transition from divine to human statement is subsequently underscored in the following paragraph where a sublimely ordered set of sentences describes the corrosive disorder at loose in the Oblonsky family, thus indicating another level where chance, disorder, and contingency reign supreme.[40]

Three levels emerge in contrast with each other: an absolute, an apparent intermediary between absolute and the relative or contingent and, then, the complete surrender to contingency. This contrast sets up a tension in the novel that is very similar to the tension between closure and openness, epic and novelistic narrative patterns in *War and Peace*. Likewise, the two main narrative trajectories of the novel have much in common with the two main trajectories of *War and Peace*, the more overtly tragic emerging in the relation of Vronsky and Anna, the more overtly comic in that between Levin and Kitty. Yet, although the similarity with Prince Andrei and Pierre seems tempting at first, it shows itself to be somewhat misleading: the structuring principle of *War and Peace* exhausts itself in *Anna Karenina* because of the latter's unrelenting focus on the overwhelming miseries of individuation, the impossibility of reconciliation between individual and totality. It is thus hardly accidental that this questioning of reconciliation takes place within a narrative having as its principal theme a violent breach of harmony brought about by what can only truly belong to the individual and which always threatens any social fabric: lust, the fervid desire for carnal pleasure that affirms the primacy of the body.

Anna Karenina is thus, as all narrative, both an exploration and representation of desire. And perhaps the most profound shift in emphasis between the two great novels consists in their different attitudes toward desire. If *War and Peace* offers the possibility that desire may be overcome, that we are not wholly trapped in the interestedness that desire expresses, our animal being, *Anna Karenina* stresses the reverse: that desire may not be overcome, that the animal will out no matter how we may wish to conceal that fact from ourselves. In doing so, *Anna Karenina* sets out an extreme indictment of desire as a negating, destructive force, as a source of inexhaustible, indomitable disquiet. Desire is endless evasion, always at variance with itself: to be itself, it must not be itself. The condition of the possibility of desire is continuous change, the impossibility of enduring satisfaction. Thus desire as the fount of action must also be that of disquiet, restlessness, the unending travail of human life that leads not to idyllic respite (no matter how ironic, as in the First Part of the Epilogue to *War and Peace*), but, rather, to the pure impossibility of stasis, of any kind of idyll other than death. In this latter sense, one might argue that *Anna Karenina* radicalizes the pessimism latent in *War and Peace*, turning the already ambiguously comic aspect of the latter into a bleak and sardonic one. The awakening of desire is a monstrous event that allows no peace, no reconciliation; rather, it is the pivotal, acrid realization of and rebellion against the individual's servitude to death, the "absolute master." *Anna Karenina* reveals the deeply tragic aspect that sheds unflattering light on the comic approach to limitation, an approach now seen almost exclusively as deception, as just another ruse with which to avoid the unacceptably bitter ache of finitude.

This frontal attack on deception, on its at once pernicious and salubrious role in the prosecution of life, is one of the most powerful aspects of *Anna Karenina* and the one that I propose to explore as a guiding approach to the dual narrative trajectories in the novel.[41] For the novel exposes the infinite negativity that is desire precisely through the endlessly inventive ways in which desire disguises that negativity from itself; in this sense, the novel's unique holism is one of artfully unmasking art as the ubiquitous and iniquitous servant of desire's self-evasion.

Ways of deceit, ways of life

As with *War and Peace*, the opening scene of *Anna Karenina* is exemplary, providing a paradigm of action that extends and repeats itself throughout the narrative. Stepan Oblonsky wakes up only to discover that he is not where he thought he was; he is thrown from a most pleasant dream into a reality that can only cause him pain, the atmosphere of tension and estrangement from his wife resulting from his indiscretion with their children's former governess. Stepan Oblonsky considers what has happened, and there is a nasty comic flavor to his process of recollection that turns between consideration of his family and his own needs as enflamed by the "dark, roguish eyes" of the governess. He cannot figure out what to do, how to confront the reality of what he has done or reconcile his competing desires. The narrator then interrupts with a striking reflection:

> There was no answer, except the general answer life gives to all the most complex and insoluble questions. The answer is: one must live for the needs of the day, in other words, become oblivious. To become oblivious in dreams was impossible now, at least till night-time; it was impossible to return to that music sung by carafe-women; and so one had to become oblivious in the dream of life. (18:1/I//6/4)

"To become oblivious" renders the Russian *zabyts'a*, "to forget oneself," and this telling phrase hangs over the rest of the novel in a remarkably pregnant manner. It is a sort of guiding metaphor inflected through many different lines of action in the narrative, both direct and oblique. In this sense, forgetfulness and deception are indistinguishable; they both describe how one turns away from what is, the unbearable truth, as a condition of living, a condition without which life would be impossible. This sounds very Nietzschean, and for good reason, because Nietzsche was, by far, the nineteenth century's most astute connoisseur of the healing powers of forgetfulness, which, for Nietzsche, achieved their highest expression in art.[42] Nietzsche insists, contrary to the traditional view, that forgetfulness is a dynamic, positive "faculty," that is at once the forerunner of the notion of repression associated with Freud and, more importantly for our purposes, a way of thinking about art, and narrative art in particular, as an active expression of forgetfulness.

Forgetfulness as a primary motive ground for action governs the two constitutive narrative trajectories of the novel with ostensibly differing results. For, as the traditional view would have it, the narrative trajectory of Anna and Vronsky is almost wholly negative, a cautionary tale of transgression and punishment. God wreaks vengeance on those who ignore (forget) his law and, of course, Anna and Vronsky do so in a flagrant, perhaps even ostentatious, way. (This severity may be somewhat leavened by the sad nature of Anna's predicament: her "tragedy" is one of a passion that can only requite itself illicitly, and so on.) Levin and Kitty form the obvious positive contrast. They are the stolidly happy couple whose virtuous and unselfish love stands as a splendid rebuke to Anna's transgression. While this contrast is well-founded in the text—it stands on the surface for all to see—upon closer inspection, the differences in outcome are much more subtly shaded, the affinity between the two narratives much more pressing and pervasive. Both Anna and Levin are stricken by the need to find forgetfulness-inducing palliatives of some kind, justifications for acting, and both ultimately do not succeed in this— as Nietzsche warns, those who pursue forgetfulness cannot forget that they are doing so—whereas Vronsky and Kitty are free of this concern: like Oblonsky, like animals, like the unborn, they share in the expansive freedom or immortality offered by limited awareness, an inherent innocence that rarely deserts them, if, indeed, it ever does.[43]

Let me clarify this contention by examining a definitive or characteristic structural aspect of each of these two narratives; namely, the patterns of forgetting that are dominant in them. Both Anna and Levin are distinguished by their inability to adhere to the illusions of order with which the grand inferential nets into which we are born ensnare us; yet both are terrified by what they see beyond them, a dark border, an abyss, infinite possibility or "a labyrinth with no center."[44] The nub of difference between the two narratives emerges in their response to this terror. For Anna's terror is admixed with an attraction to the unconditioned, its promise of freedom from the deceiving compromises of ordinary human life. She is unable to resist the radicality of the desire this attraction awakes, a desire that is uncompromising and extreme, the archetype of all desire. Levin's narrative is of quite another stamp, for, if anything, Levin's terror makes him eager to compromise, to accept (if uneasily) mediocrity as the most secure form of human existence. Anna's forgetting shapes a narrative that undoes itself by trying to give form to the all-consuming oblivion of desire—a rejection of all limits—while Levin's forgetting promotes an end of narrative, an immersion in the secure repetition of the everyday, in an illusion of timelessness akin to that of animal life wherein tradition takes the place of instinct.

Anna (and Vronsky)

Anna is caught in an impossible bind. She presents a paradigmatic picture of struggle between elegant form and those elemental forces that undermine all projections of order, all attempts to give form to nature. Form offers her forgetfulness, a rejection of the unruly energies that she keeps strictly under control—at least initially. Anna appears at the beginning of the novel as possessing assured self-control. Her movements are quick, agile, and supple. They possess the utmost grace and delicacy. She is the one who arrives to mend the breach in her brother's relation with his wife, restoring harmony and order to her brother's life. Anna wields an almost regal authority—she has triumphed over the ugliness of unchecked desire—and this authority is felt instinctively by all those who meet her, a point beautifully captured by the admiring attitude Dolly's children express to her as she sits among them, a sort of incarnate goddess:

> Whether because the children had seen that their mother loved this aunt or because they themselves felt a special charm in her, the elder two, and after them, the young ones, as often happens

with children, had clung to the new aunt even before dinner and would not leave her side. (18:1/XX//77/72)

But this authority is forced and artificial, producing a tension made clear somewhat earlier in the text when Vronsky first notices her:

> As he looked back, she also turned her head. Her shining grey eyes, which seemed dark because of their thick lashes, rested amiably and attentively on his face, as if she recognized him, and at once wandered over the approaching crowd as though looking for someone. In that brief glance Vronsky had time to notice the restrained animation that played over her face and fluttered between her shining eyes and the barely noticeable smile that curved her red lips. It was as if a surplus of something so overflowed her being that it expressed itself beyond her will, now in the brightness of her glance, now in her smile. She deliberately extinguished the light in her eyes, but it shone against her will in a barely noticeable smile. (18:1/XVIII//66/61)

This passage conveys the delicate play of tension between Anna's adherence to propriety and that "surplus of something" which she is quite unable to extinguish, or even conceal. While this play may be delicate at this point, it is fatal in the most aggressive sense of the word. Fatal because Anna's inability to affirm the claims of propriety over that mysterious, animal surplus will drive her to the complete collapse that she experiences just before she hurls herself under a train. As almost every critic and reader of the book has remarked, this fatal dimension is underscored by the horrible accident that marks Anna's arrival, for, seconds after Vronsky sees her, there is a commotion at the train station caused by the death of a train watchman, who, either drunk or oblivious, had let himself be run over by the train carrying Anna as it arrived in Moscow. Whether this death is in fact an omen or portent is open to debate, and there are compelling arguments both for and against. Yet, the mood it strikes in the novel is unmistakable—one of dread.[45] This dread is quickly forgotten, however, and all are permitted to turn away from this ugly reminder of frailty and death.

All except for Anna. Her dissolution, so powerfully governed in the novel by an animal necessity she can neither accept nor escape, is already underway. Muted flirtation with Vronsky at the ball increases her disquiet, and she seeks to return home in the hopes that her old life will protect her from the fundamental change she is undergoing: in a word, she seeks to become oblivious, to forget. But her return trip to St Petersburg—one of the dramatic highpoints of the novel— assures us that the harmony and poise she may have possessed hitherto can be maintained no longer. There are two striking, and famous, moments in the text emblematic of this change and the dangers it brings with it.

The first involves her reading an English novel. Anna imagines herself in the novel, her imagination triumphs over reason. She thereby shifts from a reality shaped by abnegation to one shaped by fulfillment of her desires. She comes closest to this latter reality when she utterly departs from the text of what she is reading. This departure is scrupulously structured in the novel—yet another case of the careful inscription of a departure from order within another order— and unfolds in roughly three stages governed by this opening comment: "Anna Arkadyevna read and understood, but it was unpleasant for her to read, that is, to follow the reflection of other people's lives. She wanted too much to live herself" (18:1/XXIX//106/100). Anna begins to imagine herself as the heroine of the text, but these imaginings soon lead her further to consider Vronsky and her feelings for him. She asks: "'What does it mean?' Am I afraid to look at it directly? Well, what of it? Can it be that there exist or could ever exist any other relations between me and this boy-officer than those that exist with any acquaintance? She smiled scornfully and again picked up the book, but now was decidedly unable to understand what she was reading" (18:1/XXIX//107/100–1). Her imaginings take on a wholly different character. They become chaotic, dispersed: they describe a sensation of "falling through the floor" or surrendering to "oblivion," a complete loss of identity:

> She kept having moments of doubt whether the carriage was moving forwards or backwards, or standing still. Was that Annushka beside her, or some stranger? "What is on the armrest—a fur coat or some animal? And what am I? Myself or someone else?" It was frightening to surrender herself to this oblivion (*zabyt'iu*). But something was drawing her in, and she was able, at will, to surrender to it or hold back from it. She stood up in order to come to her senses, threw the rug aside, and removed the pelerine from her warm dress. For a moment she recovered

and realized that the skinny muzhik coming in, wearing a long nankeen coat with a missing button, was the stoker, that he was looking at the thermometer, that wind and snow had burst in with him through the doorway; but then everything became confused again . . . This muzhik with the long waist began to gnaw at something on the wall; the old woman began to stretch her legs out the whole length of the carriage and filled it with a black cloud; then something screeched and banged terribly, as if someone was being torn to pieces; then a red fire blinded her eyes, and then everything was hidden by a wall. Anna felt as if she was falling through the floor. But all this was not frightening but exhilarating. (18:1/XXIX//107–8/101)

This brilliant, hallucinatory description gives us an Anna who has completely departed from the text, and a simple but irresistible schematic or allegorical interpretation offers itself. Anna's departure from the text, from a scripted life, is a venture into the blackness of an inchoate and dissolutive nothingness, a freedom from all enslaving objects, including the object-pretext, Vronsky. Anna is yet another Tolstoyan hero (like Olenin and Prince Andrei) who seeks freedom from all restraints, who seeks to let the imagination reign over the tedious, enslaving reality of the everyday. And this is, perhaps, the formidable terror of Anna's trajectory in the novel. Once awakened from the dreamless slumber of her everyday existence, she cannot countenance returning to it and impels herself forward to her death, for the temptation of death brings her so much closer to pure exhilaration, to a sort of communion with wilderness that leaves the everyday behind.

The latter notion comes clear in the second moment I want to discuss, the final segment of her return journey to St Petersburg when Anna finds herself facing Vronsky on the railway platform. The irony typical of this sequence in the novel is much in evidence here too, for Anna has just left the hallucinatory atmosphere of her compartment— apparently to cool off in the wintry air—only to encounter the still somewhat hidden focus of her struggles, Vronsky. This meeting is the prime matter of the following chapter, one of whose most significant characters is the snowstorm that surrounds and winds its way through the railway platform. The chapter begins with the storm:

The terrible snowstorm tore and whistled between the wheels of the carriages, over the posts and around the corner of the station.

Carriages, posts, people, everything visible was covered with snow on one side and getting covered more and more. The storm would subside for a moment, but then return in such gusts that it seemed impossible to withstand it. (18:1/XXX//108–9/102)

As Vronsky utters his fatal lines (and are they not lines?), " 'You know I am going to be where you are,' he said, 'I cannot do otherwise,' " the narrator notes:

And just then, as if overcoming an obstacle, the wind dumped snow from the roof of the carriage, blew some torn-off sheet of iron about, and from ahead a low train whistle howled mournfully and drearily. All the terror of the blizzard seemed still more beautiful to her now. He had said the very thing her soul desired but her reason feared. She made no reply, and he saw a struggle in her face. (18:1/XXX//109/102)

Now it would be the easiest thing in the world to dismiss the identification of a blizzard with passion or desire, nature's hold on us, especially in its most concentrated and accessible form, sexual desire, as hackneyed and melodramatic. But, so be it—the crudity of the metaphor fits that of which it is a figuration. Moreover, the fact that the storm threatens the stability of the platform and station house also suggests a perfectly valid figuration; namely, that Anna's passion is a destruction and abandonment of shelter. For the storm threatens to wipe away all traces of human agency, control over the animal; it describes with simple power the erotic oblivion that takes hold of Anna in the course of her love affair with Vronsky.

One may assign many names to this kind of feeling. Nietzsche memorably referred to it as Dionysian after the Greek god Dionysius.[46] But there are few better descriptions of the essential postulate than that of Edgar Allan Poe, an unlikely companion to Tolstoy:

We stand upon the brink of a precipice. We peer into the abyss—we grow sick and dizzy. Our first impulse is to shrink from the danger. Unaccountably we remain. By slow degrees our sickness, and dizziness, and horror, become merged in a cloud of unnameable feeling. By gradations, still more imperceptible, this cloud assumes shape, as did the vapor from the bottle out of which arose the genius in the Arabian Nights. But out of this *our* cloud upon the precipice's edge, there grows into palpability, a shape, far more terrible than any genius, or any demon of a tale, and yet it is but a thought, although a fearful one, and one which chills the very marrow of our bones with the fierceness of the delight of its horror. It is merely the idea of what would be our sensations during the sweeping precipitancy of a fall from such a height. And this fall—this rushing annihilation—for the very reason that it involves that one most ghastly and loathsome of all the most ghastly and loathsome images of death and suffering which have ever presented themselves to our imagination—for this very cause do we now most vividly desire it. And because our reason violently deters us from the brink, *therefore*, do we the more impetuously approach it. There is no passion in nature so demoniacally impatient, as that of him, who shuddering upon the edge of a precipice, thus meditates a plunge. To indulge for a moment, in any attempt at *thought*, is to be inevitably lost; for reflection but urges us to forbear, and *therefore* it is, I say, that we *cannot*. If there be no friendly arm to check us, or if we fail in a sudden effort to prostrate ourselves backward from the abyss, we plunge, and are destroyed. (829)

Poe calls this feeling "perverse": it entertains the forbidden merely because it is forbidden. And, while there may be an element of this in Anna's situation, the novel is extraordinarily parsimonious regarding explanations for why Anna is unable to resist the lure of Vronsky, which, in the sense I have suggested, is the lure of the unconditioned, the vertiginous, an oblivion akin to death. The critical tradition has tried on occasion to fill in the darkness with psychological speculations, an approach that is perhaps only natural given the utility of psychology and, in particular, psychoanalysis as a means of filling the darkness with light, of suggesting that there is a human "nature" with deep structures that explain away what may seem most bizarre and ineffable in human action.

Such approaches cannot but fail with Anna. For what Anna discovers is the monstrous, an abyss or void that is infinitely tempting and dangerous: it offers, with cruel irony, an incomparable and impossible freedom. From the point of view of human life, this freedom must be fatal. The temptation to attain it can only bring suffering, a longing for death, a rejection of the compromises that our limitations constantly force upon us. Not long before she throws herself under the train, Anna thinks with a new and unimpeded clarity:

"Yes, where did I leave off? At the fact that I am unable to think up a situation in life that would not be suffering, that we're all created in order to suffer, and that we all know it and keep thinking up ways of deceiving ourselves. But if you see the truth, what can you do?"

"Man has been given reason in order to rid himself of that which troubles him," the lady said in French, obviously pleased with her phrase and grimacing with her tongue between her teeth.

The words were like a response to Anna's thought.

"To rid himself of that which troubles," Anna repeated. And, glancing at the red-cheeked husband and the thin wife, she realized that the sickly wife considered herself a misunderstood woman and that her husband deceived her and supported her in this opinion of herself. It was as if Anna could see their story and all the hidden corners of their souls, turning her light on them. But there was nothing interesting there, and she went on with her thinking.

"Yes, troubles me very much, and reason was given us in order to rid ourselves of it. So I must rid myself of it. Why not put out the candle, if there's nothing more to look at, if it's vile to look at all? But how? Why was that conductor running along the footboard? Why are those young men in the other carriage shouting? Why do they talk? Why do they laugh? It's all untrue, all a lie, all deceit, all evil! . . ." (19:7/XXXI//346–7/767)

Reconciliation is impossible. There is no reconciliation, only cowardly compromise or silence. And this is the decisive discovery or moment of clarity in Anna's narrative. She cannot retreat into illusion, wear another mask that gives her some comfort for a certain period of time. To the contrary, Anna is now in a terminal position that has some similarity to that which Prince Andrei occupies on the eve of Borodino. She has come to know too much in the precise sense that she has come to realize the ephemeral quality of the bargains she has made with the desire that drives her forward. Her narrative has literally been an assemblage of lies, a slow resistance to this final realization, one that she finds unbearable. Unlike her brother, Anna is too aware to be capable of benumbing herself in the "dream of life," an awareness she tries to evade with increasingly desperate measures including the use of narcotics.

Anna's narrative undoes itself. In this final revelatory sequence, Anna sees that all narratives are evasive and palliative; they are negotiations with something that is not a thing, that can never be transformed into a thing, that refuses to give itself to us as it is. Anna sees that behind all the appearances to which we so readily attach ourselves is an absence both seductive and terrifying. She finally rejects the possibility of giving form to this absence by a supreme rejection, suicide. Like Prince Andrei in her extremity, Anna cannot resist the temptation of total freedom, of nothingness, of a complete and absolute reconciliation. Her rejection of the sedulous compromise that is everyday human life constitutes her great power and beauty.

Levin (and Kitty)

This great power and beauty is notably absent from Levin and Kitty. Theirs is a life of everyday cares: mediocre and dull, a sustained revolt against all immoderate aspiration. Where Anna is unable to resist the lure of absolute, ecstatic closure, Levin succeeds, albeit with only apparent ease. If Anna stares into the abyss and becomes one with it, Levin manages to look away. He can always find new ways of hiding, of which his greatest triumph may be his praise of the everyday. This everydayness is another form of forgetfulness, if a much more insidious and successful one than Anna's increasingly desperate evasions. It is little more than a case of that "fallenness" (*Verfallenheit*) which Heidegger derives from Nietzsche's concept of forgetfulness: a "fallen" immersion in the everyday that shields one from questions, from opening oneself to the pivotal absence that invites question, that draws one to the erotic beyond at once so terrifying and beguiling to Anna.

Levin seems clumsy, as if he, the ostentatiously natural man, does not know how to act. Levin's clumsiness is in the foreground from his first step in this society novel when he meets his good friend, Stiva. But the dinner with Stiva, which sets the tone for their subsequent meetings in the novel, is rife with irony. For Levin's clumsiness is hardly natural; it is calculated, an act that Levin carries out to express his views on the relation between the aristocracy and the peasantry, on town and country, on the complex refinements of the city-dweller as opposed to the "simple" pleasures of the country.

The theatricality of Levin's character never deserts him. Like Anna, he is continually in search of a role, and his trajectory in the novel is marked by a series of attempted transformations, from careful and benevolent landlord, to man in love (and the proper—chaste—love to boot), to upright husband and father. Each of these changes of role has its own defining, ecstatic moment, and there can be no better way of grasping the underlying pattern that emerges in them than by examining an emblematic ecstatic moment.

The famous mowing scene is characteristic. Levin has returned to his estate after his unsuccessful proposal of marriage to Kitty. In accordance with his ideas of how a landlord should comport himself with his peasants, Levin decides to help them with their mowing one day. The scene has a wonderfully light, comic atmosphere. The peasants are bewildered to see their master throw off his usual authority to sully himself in the fields. But the master insists and starts to mow along with them. He finds the work strenuous and tiring. As he becomes more absorbed in the process of mowing, he becomes less and less aware of himself as someone engaging in a particular activity. Rather, he becomes that activity:

> They finished another swath and another. They went through long swaths, short swaths, with bad grass, with good grass. Levin lost all awareness of time and had no idea whether it was late or early. A change now began to take place in his work which gave him enormous pleasure. In the midst of his work moments came to him when he forgot what he was doing and began to feel light, and in those moments his swath came out as even and as good as Titus's. But as soon as he remembered what he was doing and started trying to do better, he at once felt how hard the work was and the swath came out badly. (18:3/IV//265–6/251)

The narrator continues in the following chapter:

> The longer Levin mowed, the more often he felt those moments of oblivion (*zabyt'ia*) during which it was no longer his arms that swung the scythe, but the scythe itself that lent motion to his whole body, full of life and conscious of itself, and, as if by magic, without a thought of it, the work got rightly and neatly done on its own. These were the most blissful moments. (18:3/V//267/252)

What kind of oblivion is this? It is remarkably similar to that toward which Anna is inexorably drawn, for it, too, represents an experience of freedom, of liberation from the confines of life in time and space. But it is also quite different in that Levin experiences a harmony, a natural attunement that hints at plenitude rather than nothingness. This natural liberation is short-lived, however. As always in Tolstoy, ecstatic moments, respite from time and space, are exceedingly rare and brief: they punctuate the narrative without bringing an end to it. Time and space have too great a hold on us; our life in the world prevails unless we curtail it: the animal will out.

Levin's narrative demonstrates this latter point with delightful irony. For not long after the mowing scene, Levin sees Kitty again. His slumbering desire for her awakens, and he soon returns to his initial position in the novel, that of the anguished suitor. The difference is, of course, that Kitty accepts his proposal this time. That acceptance constitutes one of the most celebrated moments in the novel and is frequently cited as an example of Tolstoy's attachment to a sort of "nonverbal language."[47] By that I mean the miraculous way Levin communicates his hopes to Kitty and how she grasps them. Should anyone argue that a fatal element is absent from the Levin and Kitty narrative, this scene of miraculous communication puts that argument to shame. For the narrative plays on the idea of election, that two people are destined for each other, that they possess a kind of internal, animal communication unavailable to others. But this ecstatic moment of harmony is also short-lived. The rituals of betrothal take over, and Levin cuts a comic figure because the rituals so baffle and annoy him.

While Levin seems ardently to believe that his marriage will bring him some form of harmony, it does not, and he begins to grow accustomed to the thought that his wife cannot understand him. He remains uneasy, and this unease precipitates a crisis that seems to be resolved or, at least, suspended at the end of the novel. This end has a particular fascination to it because it frames Levin's journey in the novel with incisive clarity.

Levin's unease manifests itself in his seeking a justification for his life. The failure of ecstatic moments to be anything more than a brief experience of inscrutable plenitude in the fabric of lived life compels him to search out reasons for the feeling of emptiness or absence that accompanies failure. Our entrapment in time and space does not make sense to Levin. Like Anna, he cannot grasp why we are in the double bind of being imprisoned and aware of our incarceration. Levin notes: " 'Without knowing what I am and why I am here, it is impossible for me to live. And I cannot know that, therefore I cannot live' " (19:8/IX//370/788).

Levin recognizes that he cannot find answers to his questions through reason. He is thus left with either a calamitous skepticism or a friendly fiction. He chooses the latter. His friendly fiction is the tradition into which he was born, a tradition that Levin wields to take the place of reason. What do I mean? Levin's intention seems plain. After "harrowing" moments, a peasant's comment that another peasant (a certain Platon Fokanych)[48] "lives for the soul" and "remembers God" sets off a chain of thoughts for Levin. These thoughts are of a most peculiar kind, for Levin claims to understand the meaning of the peasant's words not by a process of reasoning but by another, necessarily mysterious process, a communication that is prerational and which seems to have its basis in shared tradition, in the common "soil" of tradition that brings together a particular people. Levin observes: "He lived (without being aware of it) by those spiritual truths that he had drunk in with his mother's milk, yet he thought not only without admitting those truths but carefully avoiding them" (19:8/XII//379/797). He finally criticizes reason as sly, as a swindler, and, in this, comes very close to Anna's thoughts immediately prior to her suicide.

The great difference is, of course, that Levin finds shelter from the clarity Anna achieves by returning to the tradition in which he was brought up, a tradition whose meaning he cannot however articulate—it defeats language. And this is wholly consistent with his critique of reason. All that remains is a sort of prelinguistic feeling which unites those brought up in a common tradition. Levin's narrative, then, ends with a sort of intellectual suicide, a rejection of thought in favor of feeling, a sort of capitulation before an unnamed and unnameable authority whose acceptance must be carried through by a pure, incalculable—and thus thoroughly irrational—decision.[49]

Compromise of life

Anna Karenina develops two primary narrative lines that cannot but appear ridiculous to one another, for Anna's radicalism is antithetical to Levin's conservatism. From the point of view of the radical, Levin ushers in the novel's Thermidor (something Dostoevsky instinctively grasped); he is a reactionary, one of those who reject the bold refusal of regularity, of the routine of everyday propriety. From the point of view of the conservative, Anna is a firebrand, raising dangerous passions and expectations that cannot be fulfilled in any way and which, accordingly, must result in a sort of suicide: either literal death or the figurative death of pained compromise.

One of the most brilliant facets of the novel is that it presents two deeply opposed approaches to the world, one rejecting, another appearing to accept, that comment on each other and do not end in an assuring resolution of conflict. This latter point is the crucial one and it deserves emphasis. While it may be relatively easy to claim that the line of compromise emerges victorious, I think one is ill-advised to jump to such a conclusion. What is the cost of Levin's "victory?"

Levin's "victory" is an act of surrender and, like that of Pierre in *War and Peace*, one wonders if it is durable. Certainly it is not desirable because desire is what must be offered up as a condition of surrender. Or, perhaps, that is the underlying problem with Levin's decision, for, once seen, once aroused, can the restlessness that Levin tries to quell ever be returned to a quiescent state: can it be forgotten? From this standpoint, Levin's decision is of course far less decisive than that of Anna; and, since it is so much less decisive, the question does arise as to how long it can endure.

The novel gives no answer to this question other than an implicit and unsure one. As many commentators have pointed out, the signal lack of success that Levin has enjoyed in regard to each of his attempts to reconcile himself with the absence of justification, of rationality in life, does not give a very strong assurance that he will maintain his current peace, one that requires the utter abnegation of the reflective rationality so characteristic of Levin. More telling in this regard is that Levin reaches this conclusion through an arduous process of reflection. His acquiescence to feeling is a purely intellectual, argued one, and reveals a central difficulty: How to achieve a transfer of authority from thought to feeling without in some way affirming the primacy of thought as the instrument of transfer?

The formal compromise

This problem strikes the novel as a whole, one of whose great structural ironies resides in the description of the termination or collapse of narrative order within narrative. In other words, the novel is a narrative that seeks to describe the undoing of narrative, the falsity or impossibility of narrative, and thus its own authority as a narrative.

Whereas *War and Peace* deals with the fragility of its narrative in a rather direct way, *Anna Karenina* does not. Indeed, *Anna Karenina* tends to conceal its artifice with far greater cunning than does *War and Peace*: the seams, the joints and vaults, are much more carefully hidden.[50] This is of particular interest in a work so preoccupied with forms of deception or with narratives as forms of forgetfulness of their own deep-seated impossibility. It is thus more than a little intriguing that Tolstoy referred to *Anna Karenina* as his first novel.

Is the novel, then, an act of deception? This question raises several complex and interesting issues, and they are worth examining since Tolstoy himself had much to say about the matter (and would never cease to comment on it as his major essay, *What is Art?* attests). There is a famous anecdote to the effect that, when asked to explain the meaning of *Anna Karenina*, Tolstoy replied that to do so, he would have to write the novel over again.[51] Tolstoy's response is an affirmation of the novel as inherently hostile to allegorizing, that is, to communicating essentially on two levels, one on the surface of the text, another concealed artfully below that surface. This latter kind of communication is necessarily interpretive; it involves a process of abstracting from the text, of defining various parts of it and putting them together in a new way. Tolstoy's comment flatly denies the validity of engaging in such a process, implying that it necessarily falls short of what the text seeks to say. This way of thinking is consistent with the doubts Tolstoy raises about narrative in *War and Peace*, doubts that are only obliquely voiced in *Anna Karenina*. If a narrative cannot grasp the whole, if it is already an abstraction, then how can a story about that narrative, an interpretation, be anything but a pale copy of the originating "reality?"

Yet, is it not a crucial point in *Anna Karenina* that narratives are deceptions? If that is so, then interpretations are further deceptions: they have even less reality than the original, which in itself has a reality that is necessarily inferior to its "original." In what does this latter inferiority consist? The suggestion, once again coming from *War and Peace*, is that there is no way to capture in narrative the life of all particulars, unless they exhibit adherence to a rule. Yet, if they exhibit adherence to a rule, they are in the broadest sense no longer particulars: as individuals they do not exist. *Anna Karenina* affirms this skepticism, but in a more radical way. *Anna Karenina* suggests that the life of individuals is by its very nature inscrutable, that to describe an individual is not possible. This impossibility drives Anna Karenina bewildered to her death and Levin to a sort of mysticism, an abnegation of knowledge as something that is intrasubjective for something that is inescapably, absolutely subjective and, therefore, cannot communicate itself through language. If that is so, then it follows that the novel cannot convey anything but a mask of reality as it is lived in itself, that this reality is in fact inscrutable. Therefore, the very core of what we are as individuals is unavailable to us: we can only speak by means of a generalizing language that effaces the particular in its pure particularity as a condition of giving it being.

This dilemma is in fact the crucial one exposed in both *War and Peace* and *Anna Karenina*, albeit in differing ways. We cannot know ourselves other than in the generalizing idiom of language, of public discourse. So who are we? What is this sense of being alive, of living my own life other than that which I cannot describe or which comes to me as a glaring absence? What thinks in me? Why do I choose A not B? Strictly speaking, these questions, the most pressing and powerful, cannot admit of any answer. They remain paradoxical, and as both *War and Peace* and *Anna Karenina* show with such great abundance, myriad are the ways in which characters attempt to make sense of themselves, and singular, insurmountable and monotonously conclusive is the result of their attempts: failure.

What character, what situation can give us hope? If Levin's is the final word, we have to console ourselves with impossibility. Reason seeks to confuse and beguile: no narrative, no form of communication can possibly do anything else than deceive. The deepest wells of what we are can be shared only by a kind of communication that is ineffable; in other words, about which one may not speak. The irony of this conclusion is extraordinary. Why write, if all writing is little more than an education in impossibility? Why write if all writing is tragic, an act of cruel deception that reveals only our limitations to us, that forces us into a greater silence?

This final question brings us to Tolstoy's late narrative of silence, *Hadji Murat*.

Study 4: *Hadji Murat*

Speech against silence, the garrulity of culture against the silence of nature: these are oppositions that govern the intricate multiperspectival structure of *Hadji Murat*, a novel that has received the most effusive acclaim as a pure expression of Tolstoy's narrative art.[52]

This latter designation is perhaps a good deal more astute than may seem the case, *if* one takes the opposition between language and silence as central to grasping Tolstoy's literary endeavor or, indeed, for that matter, the literary endeavor itself.

The novel begins with a transparent metaphor. The narrator struggles with a thistle, called a "Tartar," whose flower he wants to include in a bouquet he has gathered. In attempting to extract the flower for this purpose, he both hurts himself and damages the thistle. The "Tartar" is resilient, it stubbornly resists:

> When I finally plucked the flower off, the stem was already quite ragged, and the flower no longer seemed so fresh and pretty either. Moreover, in its coarseness and clumsiness it did not go with the delicate flowers of the bouquet. I felt regret at having needlessly ruined a flower which had been fine in its place, and I threw it away. "Yet what energy and life-force," I thought, recalling the effort with which I picked the flower. "How vigorously it defended, and how dearly it sold its life." (35:5–6//3)

The narrator subsequently comes across yet another "Tartar" that sticks out, mangled and disfigured, in a well-ploughed field. The narrator remarks: " 'What energy,' I thought. 'Man has conquered everything, destroyed millions of blades of grass, but this fellow refuses to surrender' " (35:6//4).

The critical reception has not been terribly kind to this metaphorical beginning.[53] The common complaint is that the metaphor is too obvious, too unsubtle: too little is left over as enticing insinuation. While the metaphor *is* obvious, that obviousness seems entirely fitting as one aspect of a text that strives to be obvious. Yet, to avoid going too far too quickly, let me take a closer look at the metaphor so that we might tease out the main elements of its obviousness, its "coarseness and clumsiness."

The opening text has two separate parts. In the first part, it is the narrator (or the implied author of the novel) who is attempting to place the flower of the "Tartar" in his bouquet. In the second part, having been unsuccessful in this attempt, the narrator sees another "Tartar" standing out in a horribly distorted form in the ploughed field, a barely living yet sturdy example of nature's resistance to man's destructive incursions. The obviousness of the metaphor, then, seems to consist in its having two layers. It is both emblematic of the author's failure to place the "Tartar" effectively in his work, the literary "bouquet" he weaves together in his text, and of a yet more consequential failure to tame nature, to capture the ever restless, recalcitrant currents of nature in the nets of reason, of form and structure—in a word, of language.

What kind of obviousness is this? Here we have a text that places a caution over itself from the very beginning, and yet in a most peculiar, indirect way, via a metaphor. There is a further hint in this: that the recourse to metaphor is perhaps necessary, for what must be told cannot be told in a direct way—or, even more to the point, that what the novel seeks to capture cannot be captured directly as it is in itself, but only indirectly via a metaphor, a way of knowing that gives us a sense of knowing more complete and integral than the novel can. To put this in different terms, metaphor supports the illusion that something can be known as a pure, timeless form, an illusion that the novel itself affirms deceptively through its brilliantly indirect narrative technique. Yet, the pursuit of direct impact through indirection points to itself—something the opening metaphor merely confirms— and thus retains the bothersome irony of the great novels, their distrust of narrative having now become cunning, indirect, silent.

Hadji Murat is perhaps the most compact and pessimistic of Tolstoy's novels in this sense, bringing the contest between the discontinuity of narrative and the continuity of its quarry to its sharpest edge. It does so, as the opening metaphor suggests, on two levels, in both the structure of the narrative and the construction of the characters.

Narrative structure

An effective way to describe the narrative structure of *Hadji Murat* is by reference to one of Zeno of Elea's famous paradoxes of motion, all of which assert the disruptive force of the infinite. The paradox I have in mind is known as "the arrow" and maintains, rather counterintuitively, that, since a flying arrow must occupy at each present moment—each "now"—a given space of equal magnitude, it must not be in motion for that precise moment, otherwise it could not occupy a given space at a given time, which is absurd. Hence, motion, which must occur in the present, is made up of a sequence of static points or "nows," and this conclusion undermines the very idea of motion.

This venerable paradox has powerful application to narrative as the description of action, bodies supposedly in motion. In this respect, the complex structure of *Hadji Murat* recalls nothing so much as a careful intrication of frozen moments, narrative pictures, or tableaux. The opening presents Hadji Murat slipping into a town at night to prepare his defection from Shamil to the Russians. The scene then shifts to a group of Russian soldiers, and from them to the ruling elements in the local imperial administration, then back again to Hadji Murat. This shifting back and forth between two defining cultural spheres, Chechen and Russian, as well as among different individuals and groups within them, is typical of the novel, which expands the contrapuntal interweaving of scenes to include Shamil himself and the Russian emperor, Nicholas I. Such shifting creates an effect of continuous discontinuity, foregrounding the discreteness of each particular scene as a picture, a "snapshot." It recalls the sophisticated mosaic of *War and Peace* and, indeed, makes a similar point, albeit in a much more condensed way. Put simply, the narrative structure of *Hadji Murat* admits the impossibility of capturing what it seeks to capture, an incident from the life of a particular individual and, through its ingenious montage technique, conveys a picture of the action that must generalize, that cannot trace the individual, the real life of events as they are in their seamless continuity. Since the narrative cannot capture continuity, it is hardly mimetic, the mere reproduction of reality, but rather a certain creation of reality.

The montage technique is also necessarily a silent commentary; it allows the author to speak indirectly in the text and does so in a manner that suggests experience is not and cannot be purely silent, that silent experience cannot qualify as experience at all. What do I mean by this? To tell a story is always an act of *re*-presentation; nothing is presented without its first being re-presented. There is no showing without telling. That is to say that no such thing as a pure or innocent narrative can exist. There are only narratives that parade or disguise their constructed nature. This is so because to have experience in the first place always indicates a gap, that there is a knower *and* a known. After all, one cannot narrate what one does not know, and there is no kind of knowledge, no piece of knowledge that is not known as such, thus, not always already deeply implicated in a web of sense. The converse makes this clearer, for how can I narrate what I do not first recognize as something for narration? Hence, all narrative is the product of re-presenting, of a structuring that assumes, but cannot present, an underlying continuity of events: syntax is sense.

What is at stake in this? *Hadji Murat* is a novel that lives and lays bare a contradiction: its narrative, as such, is inextricably linked to a way of configuring the world that indicates our ineluctable estrangement from immediacy, from the possibility of grasping things as they are and action as it is. To do so would seem to be mere reportage, but even mere reportage must succumb to omission, recasting, and modification. The life of Hadji Murat is something we cannot know other than as we construct it.

What, then, does *Hadji Murat* give us? Merely an extended metaphor, an allegory, a narrative that cannot succeed in capturing its quarry? After the complexity of the great novels, this would seem to be a meager result, especially when one considers the power and drive of the narrative, qualities that have made a tremendous impression on many formidable readers, from Isaac Babel to Harold Bloom. What *Hadji Murat* shares with its predecessors is the peculiar mix of an extremely convincing and dynamic narrative with an astonishing distrust of narrative. If anything, *Hadji Murat's* apparent perfection, its lack of narrative lecturing, of ostentatious self-awareness either on the level of the narrative or on that of the characters themselves, raises the tension between the two faces of illusion, as at once salutary and dangerous, that courses through the great novels to what is arguably its furthest extreme. In place of garrulity, one finds an eloquent and disturbing silence, whereby literature is both celebrated and taken to task for its incapacity to be anything other than a creation of reality.

Character is fate

The reality of *Hadji Murat* emerges most distinctively in its eponymous hero. But just who is Hadji Murat? The first (and usual) answer: he is a valiant warrior, a modern avatar of the heroic creations of antiquity, those heroes with which the Western literary tradition first began in the epics of Homer. While the identification of Hadji Murat with such heroes is an obvious and seemingly just one, it also has to be admitted that Hadji Murat appears to be rather more inscrutable than Achilles or Hector or Odysseus.[54] Hadji Murat is a riddle. He is pure energy and aggression, even if in his case these qualities seem to be masked by the ways in which the Russians he meets describe him. They in fact profoundly misread him, a misreading hardly surprising since it is inevitable.

Hadji Murat is difficult to read because he is always in motion. Any manner of capturing what he is may be open to revision or change. And he changes throughout the narrative, depending on circumstances. He is hardly a stable hero: what could a stable hero be after all? For Hadji Murat is heroic precisely because he is a figure of natural resistance, he does not rest, does not tame himself. This is why his surrender to the Russians cannot succeed. The Russians represent that striving to impose a final order on the world, Hadji Murat is the refusal of that striving; he is the refusal of the civilization the Russians take as the justification for their imperial ventures.

But, for all that, he is not pure nature either, since pure nature assumes civilization as its foil. Hadji Murat in his dynamism does not adhere to either definition, to either form of being. From the vantage point of the "civilized" world, his life is that of the energetic barbarian who lives by lying, killing, and destroying. The most remarkable feat of the narrative is that his violence is so attractive to the ostensibly civilized creatures that he meets. Those seduced by him are legion in the novel, and they are seduced by their longing for the wildness, both sweet and violent, he embodies and which is, strictly speaking, uninhabitable for the civilized—it is like a reflex; it is because it is.[55] Hadji Murat remains enigmatic. If obvious motivations can be ascribed to him, the only motivation which seems inconsistent with an untroubled will to survive is his concern for his family, and this motivation, both affirmation of, and departure from, his previous life, lures him to his death.

Hadji Murat is hardly the archetype of the Tolstoyan hero, unless we identify Platon Karataev as such. He is not prone to reflection, not torn by inner conflict; indeed, it is not clear if there is any inner dimension to him.[56] What drives him other than immediate concerns is not evident. He must in this sense fail to give shape to his life, for there is no governing principle to his life, he is almost wholly reactive, wholly freed of the burden of justification that so diminishes the other major Tolstoyan heroes or that makes their lives so complex and difficult. This quality invades the novel as a whole. There is no Olenin, no Andrei, no Pierre, no Levin. The characters on the Russian side are mostly selfish, using their positions as a mask for the advancement of private desires, whereas those on the Chechen side simply follow tradition or their own wants without the need for exculpatory pretexts (which, in any event, their religion provides, allowing them an additional freedom from thought).

What the novel in fact presents is a reality freed of greater purpose, a reality that in its banality, stupidity, and force is estranged from civilizing ideals—or, for that matter, any ideals at all. For ideals are those ways in which, as we have seen, we attempt to attribute to nature a benevolence in regard to human hopes that is simply absent from *Hadji Murat*. This narrative is, on the contrary, a radical assertion of fundamental estrangement: we are never at home in the world, we can never construct a world that comforts us other than as a soporific or narcotic illusion. To return to the beginning: Hadji Murat's life is an emblem of resistance to the lies that must accompany any narrative, but, as such, his life is also an acerbic commentary on the life of the energetic barbarian.

We are left, once again, to oscillate in discomfort between impossible possibilities, a life of pure dynamism that is utterly unknown to itself, that in its rigor of becoming is both brutal and senseless, or a life of futile striving, a life beset by illusions that can neither be fully denied nor tolerated. Tolstoy's final novel is disturbing precisely because it is so streamlined a questioning of attempts to create a picture of the world that will hide the ineradicable absence of ameliorative pattern or structure. For life cannot know itself other than obliquely, through illusions, shadowy creations, or projections of will, if at all. Better to be unborn, unaware, to be like Hadji Murat, freed of the need to create a narrative.

THE TOLSTOYAN NOVEL?

Tolstoy's difficulty as a novelist results from the complex crosscurrents that wax and wane in his novels, primary among which is an incredibly restless, ambivalent attitude to narrative as the creation of different possibilities of being. Most critics would admit that Tolstoy's capacity to create convincing narrative is second to none; they are much less willing to admit that his capacity to unmask narratives, to reveal their weaknesses, what they obscure or hide, seems also to have been second to none. For the most part, Tolstoy is acclaimed as one of the small number of truly great novelists. His greatness, however, is usually confined to his supposed mastery of mimesis. The clichés are legion: he creates a reality that is more real than our own, characters which we might consider as friends were they not more interesting and lively. These are the common coin of Tolstoy reception, constantly repeated and revived by students, scholars, and so-called lay readers. But it seems to me far better to say that Tolstoy is no realist in the narrow sense of re-producing a reality or, to use terms I have just employed, of re-presenting reality. Rather, Tolstoy creates a distinctive reality from the elements of common or clichéd experience. Tolstoy achieves this in a remarkable way—and this has become another, in this case, astute cliché of Tolstoy reception—by turning what is most familiar to us into what is most foreign. His novels reveal the constructed nature of our every-day reality in both cunning and obvious ways. Tolstoy is the unsurpassed master of estrangement. When the brilliant Russian critic Viktor Shklovsky referred to Tolstoy's descriptions as estrang-ing, as involving a deliberate technique of estrangement (*ostranenie*), he isolated this fundamental aspect of the Tolstoyan novel.[57]

Tolstoy is saved from banality, however, because this tendency to question is not merely negative, not merely decided in advance. The fact is that Tolstoy's narratives never decisively reject themselves. They are unparalleled in their celebration of and hostility to the arti-fice of narrative, an artifice without which life would come close to the brutish purposelessness that *Hadji Murat* gives us in the garb of an absolutely exquisitely structured, intensely questioning narrative.

If we return to the concern with truth with which I started so many pages ago, we can perhaps come to grasp that the almost fathomless complexity of Tolstoy arises from the countervailing tensions that become only more extreme in his later works. It seems to me that few writers prior to Tolstoy so candidly faced the possibility that the striving for truth must come to terms with the presence of one indubitable truth, that of the ineluctability of death, and with the terrifying absence that death strews through life, an absence beauti-fully described by Pierre Bezukhov in one of the most devastating asides in *War and Peace*:

> Sometimes Pierre remembered that he had been told about sol-diers in a shelter under fire with nothing to do, trying their best to keep busy and thus make the danger easier to bear. And Pierre pictured all men as soldiers like these, escaping from life through ambition, cards, law-making, women, little playthings, horses, politics, sport, wine, even government service. "Everything mat-ters, nothing matters, it's all the same. If I can only escape, one

way or another!" thought Pierre. "And not see *it*, the terrible *it*." (10:II/5/I//299/592)

The "terrible *it*" is death. In this evocation of the pathos of living, the pathos of "all or nothing," we can recognize a beautifully concise description of the remarkable tensions in Tolstoy's novels where all and nothing, infinite plenitude and nothingness, coexist at every moment, describing the uniquely liminal nature of human being, to be a creature that is most what it is at the interstices, in the shadowy borders between the firm conceptual categories that give those borders significance.

Perhaps even more striking is that the kind of interstitial or liminal being projected by Tolstoy's novels can neither know itself nor come to a final conclusion, remaining that "unfinished animal" of which Nietzsche wrote, one that creates and destroys out of recognition of limits, the necessity death imposes on us. That human lives consist of struggle is hardly new, that human lives are struggles to make sense of what never lends itself to sense is also hardly new. What is, however, new and extraordinary about Tolstoy's practice of the novel is the pure fecundity of struggle, the creative dynamic in which narrative comes forth as a brilliantly productive resolution to the deadlock of being that holds together briefly before again succumbing to that deadlock, an initial and imponderable freedom that flourishes only to die in a new shape of being. Freedom is interstitial being, emerging only in suspension, in an existence that does not decide. The grand, original dynamic of Tolstoy's novels describes the splendor and terror of this freedom—the openness a life can neither shape nor maintain—in ever different combinations, a necessarily infinite calculus of being.

CHAPTER 3

A FABULIST?

RADICAL NARRATIVES

Tolstoy is a superb storyteller, belonging among the most accomplished and resourceful in the Western tradition. It is possible to divide Tolstoy's production of shorter works—the novellas, longer tales, stories, and parables—into two phases, one early, one late, the dividing line being the roughly 15-year period during which Tolstoy devoted almost all his attention to the two great novels. But that is not the only distinguishing criterion, for the late short works are frequently much more austere in form and content than those Tolstoy wrote before the great novels. While this generalization, like all generalizations, can be handily dispatched by the telling counterexample, it holds good as an orienting hint to the worlds of these late short works. And I use the word "worlds" because it is quite appropriate to the peculiarly closed, perhaps even suffocating, reality that emerges in many of them. This reality arises from a further testing of fiction that extends and concentrates characteristic aspects of the great novels. If, as Milan Kundera holds, novelists are in a very broad sense explorers of the meanings of being, thus necessary contemporaries and rivals of philosophers and theologians, this quality of the novelistic endeavor seems to apply equally well to Tolstoy's late short works.[1]

In this chapter, I examine four celebrated late short works: *The Death of Ivan Ilyich*, *The Kreutzer Sonata*, "How Much Land Does a Man Need?", and *Master and Man*.[2] I have selected these four works due to their accomplished experimentalism, their sustained exploration of what fiction can be in the wake of the great novels. These are radical narratives, they go to the roots of fiction by confronting themes that represent the constrictive arm of necessity in human life: in this sense, they are almost obsessively repetitive, like necessity itself. For if one may well quibble with the notion that there is some fixed human nature, a paradigmatic model of what it is to be human that must be accepted if we are to be human—that is, another form of that coercion which has been considered both necessary and intolerable in the prosecution of communal existence—it is much harder to suggest that there are no decisive conditions of human life. Death, sex, evil, and inequality, the main themes of the narratives I have selected, all possess this decisive character: they direct a challenge to us that requires a decision, a narrative response.

DEATH

To begin with the end is only appropriate. This is at least what *The Death of Ivan Ilyich* dares to do. The plot is revealed in the first few lines: " 'Gentlemen,' he said, 'Ivan Ilyich is dead' " (26:I//61/3).[3] The breach in ordinary narrative progression that the beginning seems to offer is a sardonic analogy to death and the role of death as the end of all narratives.[4] But there is yet another dimension to this piece of narrative cunning, for the beginning also sets out the story's major themes in a remarkably concentrated manner. If we liken *The Death of Ivan Ilyich* to a musical work, we might argue that the beginning is a sort of overture in which all the significant elements of the ensuing drama are carefully announced.

Principal among these is the treatment of necessity in its most formidable guise, death, as something that at all costs must be evaded. In a way fully consonant with *Anna Karenina*, the beginning describes the dominant pattern of the story, whereby the truth, that awful truth of death, briefly comes to light only to be suppressed again through a web of deceptions. Life without lies is intolerable; and the lies in this case are of the most fundamental sort, they convince us that we are free, that we can dispose over the material conditions of our existence as we see fit. Moreover, the stark simplicity of the story matches that of its subject matter: complication emerges only in the response to it, in the desperate ingenuity of deception that founds the possibility of living.

Beginning at the End

Let us take a close look at how the story's beginning frames this idea. The setting is a law court, a place of judgment, suggesting a malicious allusion to the last judgment (*strashnii sud*). The officials, all colleagues of Ivan Ilyich, are discussing various matters when one of them finds the announcement of Ivan Ilyich's death in a newspaper and informs the others. With delightfully heavy-handed malice, the narrative gives us their thoughts:

> So when they heard of the death of Ivan Ilyich, the first thought of all those present in Shebek's chambers was how this might affect their own relocations and promotions, and those of their friends.
>
> "Now I'll probably get Shtabel's place or Vinnikov's," thought Feodor Vassilievich. "It's been promised to me for a very long time. The promotion will bring me a raise of eight hundred rubles, apart from the allowance for office expenses."
>
> "I'll have to put in for my brother-in-law's transfer from Kaluga," thought Piotr Ivanovich. "My wife will be very pleased. And no one can say I never did anything for her relatives."
>
> "I thought he'd never get up from his bed again," said Piotr Ivanovich aloud. "Very sad." (26:I//61–2/4)

The officials think only about their own affairs when they hear of Ivan Ilyich's death. The obvious interpretation is that these are callow people unable to consider anything without foregrounding their own interests, this being particularly ironic since they are presumably called frequently to pass judgment with impartial rigor on the disputes that come before them. But the more probing irony is that the immediate turn to selfish concerns is the necessary way of life, the reaction of a vital, living being to the intolerable: it is, in a word, deception. And, as deception, it is particularly ironic because the foremost interest of the mortal creature must be death. But this interest, it seems, can best be protected or maintained through evasion, a forgetting of limits that would otherwise freight life with too much despair: *respice finem* is not for the living.

It is thus predictable that the officials all seek a pretext for changing the topic, and this is provided by Piotr Ivanovich who complains that he lives far away from Ivan Ilyich, making the social duty of funeral attendance that much more cumbersome. "The conversation passed to the distances between different parts of the city, and they went back into court" (26:I//62/4). The disturbing news is swept away along with the "happy feeling that he is dead, not I" (26:I//62/4).

Animal vitality brooks no communication with death; and, indeed, if evasion of death is immediate and instinctual—there is no suicide in the animal world, at least as far as we know—why should that evasion not extend in the broadest way to society and its institutions, which are not designed to terminate but to promote human life?[5] In this respect, there is perhaps no social order more committed to aiding and abetting animal comfort than the bourgeois order to which Ivan Ilyich strives to belong.

The funeral, into which this opening scene merges almost seamlessly, is perhaps even starker in its depiction of evasion; as such, it is the centerpiece of the beginning chapter, if not the entire story. Tolstoy has received scant praise as a humorist, and this is quite unjust, since the depiction of the funeral is worthy of Beckett in its economy, savagery, and pitiless loathing of human subterfuge. Piotr Ivanovich arrives, and a friend, Schwartz, winks at him "suggesting, as it were, 'Ivan Ilyich has made a real mess of things, not like you and me'" (26:I//63/5). What a telling admission! The active verb underlines a crucial element of deception, assuming that Ivan Ilyich might have had a choice. But, of course, the thought that one can choose not to die is absurd. It only reveals a residue of deeply entrenched and mendacious assumptions about human agency, a sort of ragged life preserver for the slowly drowning.

While Schwartz tries to arrange a game of cards for that evening, a jolly pastime, Piotr Ivanovich enters into the room where Ivan Ilyich's open coffin is placed for all to see. He enters, "as one always does, in total uncertainty over what he should do when he got there" (26:I//63/5). This uncertainty is mordant. After all, what does one do in the face of death? And what can bring one closer to the irreducible reality of death than a waxen corpse? Piotr Ivanovich decides to cross himself out of perplexity, and this reflex is a wonderfully offhand allusion to the function of religion in face of the uncertainty about death: better some coating of ritual than nothing at all. Piotr Ivanovich then looks at Ivan Ilyich's body:

He had grown much thinner and was considerably changed since Piotr Ivanovich last saw him, but his face, as with all the dead, was more beautiful and, more important than that, more meaningful than it had been in his lifetime. The expression on the face suggested that what needed to be done had been done, and done as it should be. Moreover, the expression held a rebuke or reminder to the living. Such a reminder seemed to Piotr Ivanovich to be out of place here, or at least of no relevance to him. He became rather uncomfortable, somehow. He hastily crossed himself again—too quickly it seemed to him, without due regard for the appropriate courtesies, and turned to leave. (26:I//64/6)

Piotr Ivanovich does his best to ignore that reminder or rebuke. He is buoyed by Schwartz, who "rose above such things and did not succumb to unpleasant impressions" and whose appearance proclaims that "there are, in short, no grounds for thinking that this episode can stop us spending the evening as pleasantly as possible" (26:I//64/6). These statements are indelicate provocations, and that is precisely the point: the rancid theatricality of the funeral scene, the careful rituals, the way the body is arrayed with a peaceful, no doubt serene expression, are all elements in the work of deception that surrounds death, a work of deception that spirals into inanity.

Inanity reaches its height in the conversation between Piotr Ivanovich and Ivan Ilyich's wife, Praskovya Feodorovna. One of Tolstoy's favorite devices, an unruly object, speaks more eloquently than the characters themselves, this surely being a rude inversion, since the insentient gives voice to what the sentient would prefer to keep hidden. This object is an ottoman that stirs and creaks throughout Piotr Ivanovich's conversation with Praskovya Ivanovna. The ottoman provides a comic commentary on Piotr Ivanovich's hapless efforts to listen earnestly to the widow's pious laments—most of which are drenched in self-pity—and to make his own inquiries, as one is supposed to do, about the last days of his erstwhile friend. Soon this absurd conversation, an inelegant play of duplicity, turns toward the real issue, Praskovya Ivanovna's concern about "how much money she might get from the Treasury on her husband's death" (26: I//67/9).

Only Piotr Ivanovich's brief exchange with Gerasim offers relief. Gerasim's attitude to death—"God's will. We'll all come to that"— sounds a different note: it is simple and direct, another echo of the peasant "wisdom" of Platon Karataev and Platon Fokanych (if not that of Uncle Eroshka and Hadji Murat as well). Moreover, in contrast to the lugubrious dissimulation that prevails at the funeral, with almost everyone trying to divert their attention from the matter at hand, Gerasim moves swiftly and with purpose. He does not find himself at a loss but is engaged in basic, essential tasks.

This blackly comic beginning establishes the pattern of evasion that predominates in the ensuing narrative, and it does so with blunt, ferocious irony. But it also goes one step further, anticipating a conclusion easily drawn from the subsequent narrative: that Ivan Ilyich's death is far more important and interesting than his life, that his death is the most properly definitive aspect of his life, and, perhaps, not only of his life.

The Bourgeois Dream

The succeeding chapters of the story present one of the most profoundly disturbing nightmares in world literature, a narrative whose end is indubitable, whose power comes from absolutely ruthless patience and descriptive acumen. If the beginning of the story shows a pattern of evasion, the narrative of Ivan Ilyich's life and slow death is a deftly ironic play on narrative itself as a means of evasion. For this narrative reveals the horrifying and banal truth, which the other narratives set out in the story seem otherwise designed to conceal. The primary narrative thus brings to ruin the pretensions of narrative as a form of justification in a way that recalls *Anna Karenina* but casts aside that work's attempt at a final reconciliation, no matter how frail and unconvincing. The far-reaching significance of *The Death of Ivan Ilyich* as a short work lies in its uncompromising attitude toward the pretensions of narrative and, in particular, the multiform narratives of the great novels. The austere style, the compactness, the singularity of purpose, that dominate *The Death of Ivan Ilyich* reject in practice what the great novels sought to pursue with tenacious ambivalence. And this is characteristic of the late fiction, as we shall see.

The first lines of this narrative are justly famous: "The past history of Ivan Ilyich's life was simple, commonplace, and most terrible" (26: I//68/11). The brief account that follows—only 2 chapters out of 12—proceeds under the shadow of this judgment: Why exactly was Ivan Ilyich's past life terrible? At first, Ivan Ilyich's life appears exemplary or enviable, the kind of life to which many aspire. He was well-liked and built a successful career. He had adventure, moved about the country, found favor with women, married a beauty, and set himself and his wife up in abundance, as do "all those people who are not quite rich enough, who want to look like the rich, and consequently look only like each other" (26:III//79/22). From the outset,

Ivan Ilyich aims to satisfy his material needs and is fortunate enough to be able to do so. He is the picture of bourgeois health, the well-trained insider who manages to secure his position in the privileged echelons of society. What more could one want? What is terrible about this life? For is this not a life that has achieved freedom from terror? Is it not "pleasant and proper" as the narrator repeats time and again?

The obvious objection here, one dear to the enemies of bourgeois comfort, is that Ivan Ilyich seems inert as an individual.[6] He simply does what all do. He makes sure that he does not stick out, that he is neither too *this* nor too *that*. In short, Ivan Ilyich represents a life lived in harmony with his world, a life that is content and, in this sense, happy. The enemies of bourgeois comfort reject such a life, and they do so based on a simple accusation: that the primary condition of such a life is deception, that such a life can only achieve the harmony and comfort it seems to achieve by concealing anything that might disturb that harmony. Of course, that disturbance will make itself known one day or another, revealing the abject falsity of a life that has tried to evade such things. I am reminded here of the Beckett play "Happy Days" where the main character, Winnie, cheerfully (and, thus, obliviously) warbles away about her day-to-day activities while imbedded in a mound that comes up to above her waist. The astringent point there matches that of *The Death of Ivan Ilyich*: life is not lived pleasantly and properly, other than through some form of distraction, and those who seek to make it so—and who does not, after all?—must seem ridiculous.

There is, however, a greater conflict at work here. Any society must demand that its members conform, that they give up their individuality to a comprehensive collective subjectivity. Even supposedly tolerant, pluralistic, liberal democratic societies do this, only in ways that are generally more complicated and refined than their often brutal counterparts. Hence, the question arises as to whether the conformism of Ivan Ilyich, given its inevitability, is malignly deceitful by definition or whether the particular society in which Ivan Ilyich finds himself, this being the society of the bourgeois, imposes that sort of deceit. It is not clear that the story offers an answer to this question. Those critics who argue that the story attacks only a certain kind of society, specifically that of a particular era and class structure, hold up Gerasim as the positive, hopeful alternative to the world of Ivan Ilyich.[7] There is something to this argument, which affirms the rude traditions of the peasant world that are "bred in the bone" or "drunk in with one's mother's milk"—in other words, traditions that, in the abeyance of thought, provide a worthy substitute for instinct— against the society of the professional, the doctor or lawyer or urban planner, to which Ivan Ilyich belongs.

But I think that this approach to the story misses another important question that the narrative poses merely by relating the facts of Ivan Ilyich's life as it does. It seems to me far too easy simply to dismiss Ivan Ilyich as a superficial bourgeois, leading an empty life. By doing so, the broader question may be avoided: is a life without deception possible? This is the question that the narrative itself poses to the extent it lays bare the misery of Ivan Ilyich's slow recognition that he is dying and cannot return to his pleasant life. This portion of the story is its core. Nine chapters that describe with devastating simplicity Ivan Ilyich's coming to recognize his own mortality, whereby he attains a sobriety from the intoxication of life's many deceptions that may be impossible to tolerate. This question, of whether death can ever be tolerable for the living, constitutes the challenge of the story, and it applies to all regardless of social standing. To think in this way is to look at Gerasim differently and to question whether his peasant wisdom offers any better solution to the insoluble dilemma of death.

The Bourgeois Nightmare

What I refer to as the "nightmare" begins with chapter IV and runs to the end of the story. This is by far the most striking and powerful part of the story, a narrative of brute necessity, of the gradual recognition that there is no escape, no release, no freedom from pain and death. The asphyxiating atmosphere of these chapters results from several remarkable features of the narrative, its temporality, its increasing concentration and the isolation of Ivan Ilyich. I should like to discuss each of these aspects of the narrative in turn.

As several critics have noted, the chapters in this section of the story become shorter and shorter.[8] This tendency reflects how Ivan Ilyich's sense of time begins to change as he comes closer to the realization of the inflexible nature of his illness, its fatal resistance to human manipulation. The primary aspect of this change is an apparent acceleration that becomes an almost complete stasis toward the end, when Ivan Ilyich ceases to recognize time anymore. To conceive of time in broadly elastic terms has notable precedents in Tolstoy's works, particularly in *Anna Karenina*, where a different temporal signature underscores the differing trajectories of the two main pairings. In *The Death of Ivan Ilyich*, the changing perception of time is a significant index articulating Ivan Ilyich's response to his illness. If time moves slowly or imperceptibly at first, maintaining its discreet distance as an immediate reality or given of his life—indeed, the only given—it becomes more perceptible as a headlong rush toward an undesired, fearsome end before it finally subsides; the effect is one of a wave slowly building up only to crest and falter against the shore.

Zeno of Elea's celebrated paradox suggesting motion is an illusion, that of Achilles and the tortoise, offers a perhaps more telling metaphor.[9] The paradox works as follows: suppose that Achilles can run ten times faster than the tortoise and generously gives the tortoise a ten-meter head start in the race. Achilles runs ten meters, the tortoise one; Achilles runs that meter, the tortoise a further decimeter; Achilles runs that decimeter; the tortoise a centimeter; Achilles runs that centimeter; the tortoise a millimeter, and so on to infinity. No matter how far Achilles runs, he is never capable of overtaking the tortoise.

The situation the paradox describes, one where there is constant motion toward an ever receding goal, motion that is thus static, thus only apparent, is characteristic of the peculiar structure of the final chapters where time seems to accelerate but, in effect, never gets closer to its goal: so long as there is time, original plenitude and luxury, there is life, and life, having become increasingly agonizing and cruel, does not end. It is only in the final chapter of the story that Ivan Ilyich makes the qualitative jump from time to what is beyond time—"there is no more death" (26:XII//113/59), since death as a terminus can have no further meaning or coherence for one who has reached that end.

This peculiar sense of time is complemented by Ivan Ilyich's increasing isolation from those around him.[10] Isolation is the operative metaphor describing the fundamental change of perspective that takes place in Ivan Ilyich, perhaps best addressed as one whereby Ivan Ilyich begins to see his previous life as a tissue of lies that becomes intolerable in the face of death. If time was once the preserve and resource of being, only to become that of death, likewise the "pleasing and proper" society which once provided the joyous milieu of Ivan Ilyich's life, becomes a cruel reminder, a network of deception or "screens" that Ivan Ilyich sees with pellucid clarity in the face of death. The narrator takes care to emphasize this point:

> Ivan Ilyich suffered most of all from lies—the lie that everyone accepted, for some reason, that he was just ill, not dying, that he need only keep calm and take his medicine and something splendid would come of it. And he knew that whatever the medicines might do, nothing would come of it except more agonizing misery and death. He found the lie insufferable; he was tormented by the fact that nobody wanted to admit what he knew—what everyone knew—but chose to lie to him about his dreadful state. They wanted, even forced him to participate in the same lie. Lying, the lie inflicted on him on the eve of his death, the lie which was bound to degrade the fearful, solemn scene of his death to the level of all those visits, curtains and sturgeons for dinner . . . this was a dreadful affliction for Ivan Ilyich. (26:VII//97–8/42)

The lie is dreadful because it isolates him from all those surrounding him and emphasizes the gulf growing between him and them, the gulf that separates the dying from the living. For the living cannot of course live without the lies they create and perpetuate; lying is their condition of life without which the latter would be intolerable.[11] Hence, Ivan Ilyich's rejection of the lie not only is a sharp admission of the immediate reality of his terminal state, it is also a poignant and sober realization of the qualitative difference that by its very nature must isolate him: for how can the living understand or appreciate his terminal thinking? Indeed, how can the reader grasp what the others can or will not?

Ivan Ilyich responds to this qualitative difference by seeking distance from those around him, most of whom are only too happy to grant his wish. He seeks more spare surroundings so that he might forget the material instantiation of that world, the proper furniture, and so on. Just like the people, the objects of his past life remind him of lies, in this case the false sense of power and permanence that ownership implies. This is surely a ferocious indictment of the illusions of ownership. Since I shall deal with this issue in greater detail below (in my examination of "How Much Land Does a Man Need?"), I want merely to suggest here that ownership can be a kind of secularized immortality; to possess property, to have control over things, gives one the illusion of attaining to an authority that would otherwise be associated with the deity. For what can ownership possibly mean, if there is nothing that is truly mine, nothing that I can possess that has any chance of lasting? Is not absence the identity of my proper "I," that which thinks in me and ebbs away?

Ivan Ilyich's horrible and unrelenting pain speaks to this absence. Not only does Ivan Ilyich's pain isolate—for, as Wittgenstein notes, how can one ever communicate pain?[17]—it also eliminates all residue of thought, it hollows out, it dominates, it is the voice and herald of nothingness. This may sound like poetic fancy, but pain is in a radically excessive way the presence of that nothingness, that ineffable individuality of embodiment, which indicates the elusiveness of identity. Pain is a constant reminder that one's identity cannot be communicated, and, in the deadly ironic manner of the story, pain asserts what cannot come to language.

Gerasim is the riddle in the wake of this interpretation. What is it about Gerasim that so pleases and cheers Ivan Ilyich through his worst nights? What distinguishes Gerasim from the others? If we take the problem of the lie as central, Gerasim seems to be distinguished by the fact that he is not prone to it. Gerasim resembles a sort of Candide whose "countenance expressed his soul," to cite Voltaire's memorable phrase. Gerasim does not dissimulate, there is no disastrous separation between exterior and interior as there is with all the other characters in the story. To the contrary, Gerasim possesses the unity of innocence, and this unity seems to be highly valued by Ivan Ilyich and highly resistant to the despair that leads the others to choose various kinds of screens to protect themselves, albeit feebly, from Ivan Ilyich's death.

While Gerasim is the only character who is able to speak of death, to do what needs to be done without the screens which all the others must deploy from time to time as a condition of being able to live, there is also no doubt that he is, at best, a vague character, perhaps almost a caricature, a child, an innocent. His welcome presence seems to have no greater importance or force than Ivan's recollections of his childhood as a time when he had not yet become entrapped in the compulsory lies of his social compact. And there is a certain irony in the fact that Ivan Ilyich chooses to sequester himself with such a person, since Gerasim's childlike freedom from deception is an emptiness not wholly dissimilar to that which Ivan Ilyich comes increasingly to feel in the face of death.

Death

The final three chapters of *The Death of Ivan Ilyich* have occasioned considerable debate, much of which concerns the elusive "black bag" or "black sack" (*chernii meshok*), a metaphor at once transparent and ambiguous:

> It seemed to him that he and his pain were being painfully pushed into a long, narrow black-sack, pushed in deeper and deeper, and yet could not be pushed right through. And this terrible business is agonizing for him. He is both afraid, and wants to fall through; he struggles against it, and he tries to help. And suddenly he tore free, and fell, and came to himself. (26:IX//105/50)

The metaphor is an apt emblem of the narrative that precedes it; a sort of narrowing that is also a paradoxical widening; constriction that is expansion as well. This paradoxical duality is extremely characteristic of the last three chapters which define a pattern that plays off rejection of his past life against a longing to return to it. To the extent this longing prevails, Ivan Ilyich holds to life and does not make the final leap. It is important to note that an unresolved question—"Why have you done all this? (26:IX//105//50)—seems to hold Ivan Ilyich to life, hardly a surprising result given the devotion to life, to finding or creating a solution, that is typical of any fundamental question.

But this question is never answered clearly, something that those attached to ameliorative or overtly Christian accounts of Ivan Ilyich's death seem to pass over in silence. They can point to an important paragraph in the last chapter where Ivan Ilyich realizes that his life "can still be put right" even at the end. This is no doubt a tempting admission, if one seeks to impose a Christian interpretation: here we have the penitent sinner who, upon realizing the vapidity of his life, finally comes to accept that fact, thereby saving himself. Recognition is equivalent to salvation. It would be wrong to dismiss this interpretation out of hand. But if the Christian interpretation should not be ruled out as one possible view, it likewise should not rule out other approaches that proceed in a different direction. Among these, one might look at this moment in the text as caustically ironic, expressing something closer to a heroic, Socratic perspective, namely that Ivan Ilyich puts right his prior life simply by discarding its intricate lies and facing death, accepting death. In this sense, death is no more, because, once faced or accepted, it ceases to possess that all-encompassing force that compels people into subterfuge, that makes death the utterly unacceptable, "hidden king" in life.

SEX

The Kreutzer Sonata is one of Tolstoy's most extreme and, in regard to form, least characteristic works. For many who admire the artistic mastery of Tolstoy, the work seems to be a failure, an unacceptable breach of the mimetic compact where the need to expound a fanatic message drowns out the subtler pleasures of art. But I think that this position is based, ironically enough, on a peculiar, but telling, misapprehension of the work's cunning artistry. For *The Kreutzer Sonata* is in large part a confession framed by an orienting narrative. It is the confession of a murderer. The views that have most excited opposition and disgust emerge in the context of that confession; this fact alone should advise some caution regarding interpretation of them as pronouncements of a cantankerous author.[13]

The story begins on a train, and, specifically, with a discussion on a train that describes differing attitudes to marriage. This opening offers rich opportunities for facile allegorizing: the discussion brings together two different social orientations, one progressive, as represented by the lawyer and the "no longer young" lady, the other conservative, as represented by the merchants. The main character in the story, Pozdnyshev, belongs to neither tendency. He is beyond both as befits a murderer, one who has rejected the bounds of society. That the discussion takes place on a train suggests a society in motion, in the process of change. When Pozdnyshev takes over the narration, this notion of change becomes quite ironic: Pozdnyshev's narrative is a journey into the final madness of murder, of the negation of social order.

The discussion itself concerns the concept of marriage. The progressive view presents marriage as the societal consecration of love. The conservative view leans to a concept of marriage as an obligation that may well serve other, baser interests. From this latter standpoint love, the justification for marriage according to the progressive view, has far less significance. The discussion does not get too far. The arguments on both sides seem to pass by each other, as if to say that arguments challenge little and convince even less. Pozdnyshev's "confession" narrative encourages this impression, for here is a narrative that labors to convince more by the power of its captivating radicality and apparent sincerity than by the merit of its arguments.

Journey to the End of the Night

Pozdnyshev's narrative starts with a series of provocative arguments. They act as a sort of prelude to his direct account of how he killed his wife. The narrative thus moves from the general to the particular, from arguments that claim to hold equally of all to the most direct proof of the validity of those arguments in his own life. This movement is hardly innocent; it suggests that Pozdnyshev is creating a justification for the murder, that his recourse to the tools of rational discourse merely conceals the orientation of that discourse to his own, largely exculpatory, ends.

His opening arguments are by now familiar Tolstoyan territory. They assume that society is largely deceptive, that it permits subterfuge through the institution of marriage, an institution concealing uncomfortable realities. Pozdnyshev speaks plainly:

> "But you're talking all the time about physical love. Don't you acknowledge love based on identity of ideals, on spiritual affinity?" asked the lady.
>
> "Spiritual affinity! Identity of ideals!" he repeated, emitting his peculiar sound. "But in that case why go to bed together? (Excuse my coarseness!) Or do people go to bed together because of the identity of their ideals?" he said, bursting into a nervous laugh. (27:I//14/179)

Pozdynshev attacks the premise that ennobles and sanctifies marriage as a spiritual bond, the unification of two souls. This premise assumes, in accordance with Christian dogma, that the soul is more valuable than the body, that the spirit is greater than the flesh. But Pozdnyshev subverts this valuation, maintaining that it merely masks the far greater authority of the body, a reality that we would prefer not to confront. This reality is uncomfortable because it points to our finitude, to our desperate vulnerability, to desire's claim on us.

The overwhelming desire for sex, and, specifically, that of the male, creates vulnerability in this case. This desire reaffirms the essential selfishness of the body—my desire must take precedence over consideration of others. It follows that others are nothing more than instruments of satisfying this desire, they have no existence for me apart from their function. But these others tend not to be willing instruments of satisfaction, and that is why society offers mendacious pretexts through which selfish desire may achieve satisfaction unchecked. Pozdnyshev is eager to unmask this aspect of society which, by his lights, promotes "freeing oneself from moral relations with a woman with whom you have physical intimacy." Pozdnyshev continues: "Such emancipation I regarded as a merit. I remember how I once worried because I'd not had an opportunity to pay a woman who gave herself to me (having probably taken a liking to me) and how I only calmed down after having sent her some money— thereby intimating that I didn't consider myself morally bound to her in any way" (27:III//17/181). At issue here is morality as a means of overcoming selfish prerogatives. To use well-known (Kantian) terms, Pozdnyshev assumes that morality demands we consider others as ends in themselves and not as means to ends that we wish to pursue.[14] To comply with these demands is to relinquish the material interests of the body in favor of perfect disinterest, either as complete abandonment or subjugation of such material interests. Pozdnyshev's argument assumes this point of view but denies that it can be realized in practice. For him, the interests of the body must prevail.

Pozdnyshev's most radical argument for this claim relates to the "natural" end usually given as a justification for sex, the continuation of the species. For Pozdnyshev dares his interlocutor to explain why reproduction is necessary, and this brings up the central question of why it is so important that there be human beings. It is noteworthy that immediately before Pozdnyshev poses this question, he objects to the light in the carriage and shades it. There is no subtlety here, but the progression into darkness is apposite. Pozdnyshev's remarks, worth quoting at length, reveal the fundamental axis of the work:

"Natural?" he replied. "Natural? No, I may tell you that I've come to the conclusion that it is, on the contrary unnatural. Yes, quite *un*natural. Ask any child, ask an unperverted girl."

"Natural you say!"

"It's natural to eat. Eating is, from the very beginning, enjoyable, easy, pleasant, and not embarrassing; but this is horrid, shameful, and painful. No, it's unnatural! And an unspoilt girl, as I have convinced myself, always hates it."

"But how," I asked, "would the human race continue?"

"Yes, wouldn't the human race perish?" he replied, irritably and ironically, as if he'd expected this familiar and insincere objection. "Teach abstention from child-bearing so that English lords may always gorge themselves—that's all right. Preach it for the sake of greater pleasure—that's all right; but just hint at abstention from child-bearing in the name of morality—and, my goodness, what a rumpus . . . ! Isn't there a danger that the human race may die out because they want to cease to be swine? But forgive me! This light is unpleasant, may I shade it?" he said, pointing to the lamp. I said I didn't mind; and with the haste with which he did everything, he got up on the seat and drew the woolen shade over the lamp.

"All the same," I said, "if everyone thought this the right thing to do, the human race would cease to exist."

He did not reply at once.

"You ask me how the human race will continue to exist," he said, having sat down again in front of me, and spreading his legs far apart he leaned his elbows on his knees. "Why should it continue?"

"Why? If not, we shouldn't exist."

"And why should we exist." (27:XI//29/191)

The frame narrator is unable to respond to this challenge other than by saying that we should exist "in order to live." Characteristically, Pozdnyshev counters this response with a question about the purpose of life. For to live merely to live is hardly sufficient for him: he needs to know why.

Pozdnyshev shows his hand. He belongs among those who demand that life justify itself, and he does so in the face of the obvious evils in life, prime among which is our mortal limitation. If our mortal limitation is the author of all our woes and, in particular, the "tragedy of the bedroom," then it is hard not to demand why we are so built, indeed, why the world is so built.[15] For the tragedy of the bedroom is not merely exhausted by the desire for sex in itself, but also by the corresponding desire to secure the availability of satisfaction for as long as possible; in other words, for the retention of an instrument of satisfaction in perpetuity that allows a sense of ownership or mastery the incessant need itself belies. If that mastery is, however, impossible, death is to be preferred. What is at stake here?

Pozdnyshev's argument may be summarized as follows. Society is a pretext. It conceals a commitment to selfish pleasure, individual desire, rather than the being of the species. Indeed, the striving to transform sex through birth control solely into a means of obtaining pleasure is the rejection of species being in favor of my being. Otherwise, the sexual impulse reveals us to be mere pawns of nature's cunning, for nature gives us fleeting pleasure in exchange for continuance of ends which we cannot claim to understand. Hence, the restriction of sexual relations to those of unalloyed pleasure thwarts nature, turning exchange into a meager profit. For one not satisfied with this meager profit, for one who seeks to extirpate sexual desire entirely, the results also entail thwarting natural ends, a rather biting irony given the apparent intent of Pozdnyshev's argument. In either case, the consequences are the same: the species dies with the individual, a death that constitutes an act of revenge for the subordination of individual mortality to species immortality.[16] For why should we exist exclusively to promote ends we can neither understand nor come to accept?

The tale that ensues emphasizes the cruelty that leads Pozdnyshev to such desperate arguments. Pozdnyshev cannot renounce his sensuality, and his desire to secure his object of satisfaction is extreme. That he fears he cannot secure that object, his wife, leads him to wild transports of jealousy; the upshot of the remaining narrative is that Pozdnyshev's jealousy reveals, in perhaps an extreme way, the essential contours of the "tragedy of the bedroom," a tragedy that is enacted in some form in all marriages, which are nothing more than proprietary relationships permitting the usufruct of a valuable asset for both parties, but, as Pozdnyshev never tires of pointing out, ultimately for the advantage of the male.

The Eroticism of Art

One of the most important aspects of this story is the role of art in it. Beauty, once the standard by which works of art were judged, has an unambiguous status in Pozdnyshev's narrative. Contrary to Platonism, which identifies beauty with the good and the true, Pozdnyshev regards beauty as corrupting: "It's amazing how complete the delusion is that beauty is goodness" (27:V//21/184). In one of the fundamental reversals that characterize the story, beauty loses its status as spiritual ideal, as raising the earthbound creature to the higher realm of the ideas, to become a force of corruption and the foremost expression of the lie. For beauty pretends to inculcate a love of the ideal when it in fact merely ignites baser passions: beauty aids the cunning of nature.

This beauty is essentially that of the tart, the demonic seductress, and it serves Pozdnyshev well in his argument against society:

> "That's why there are those detestable jerseys, bustles, and naked shoulders, arms, almost breasts. A woman, especially if she has graduated from the male school, knows very well that all the talk about elevated subjects is just talk; what a man wants is her body and all that presents it in the most deceptive and alluring light, and she acts accordingly. If we only throw aside our familiarity with this indecency, which has become second nature to us, and look at the life of our upper classes as it is, in all its shamelessness—why it's simply a brothel . . . You don't agree? Allow me, I'll prove it," he said, interrupting me. (27:VI//22-23/186)

Pozdnyshev's account of his courtship and marriage is the proof, at least the initial one. For Pozdnyshev is seduced by his wife's beauty, by the sensual delights she seems to promise for him. These delights are incapable of sustaining a marriage, however, and Pozdnyshev spends a good deal of time making the argument that their marriage could not survive on sensuality alone. Indeed, a pattern develops where moments of calm, always preceded by sex, give way to increasingly frequent bouts of aggravation on both sides. This aggravation works out into a tormenting jealousy. For, once his wife has given up the grueling task of reproduction, she seems to become more alluring than ever and, without the risk of pregnancy, Pozdnyshev begins to attribute to her the traits of a potential predator, an animal capable of coupling with any number of men. This thought begins to haunt Pozdnyshev; his need to assert his own dominance and authority, the prerogatives of his body, leads to an ever more agitated jealousy, a spreading fear that he may not be able to have exclusive rights over his wife's body. The immediate causes of this jealousy are not clear. One has to assume that they relate to his wife's freedom from the burdens of reproduction, but also from Pozdnyshev's firm belief in the triumph of the animal, a belief that may indeed apply more to himself than his wife.

The catalyst for the looming disaster is, of course, music. Pozdnyshev's putative rival is a musician, "not a professional, but a semi-professional semi-society man" (27:XIX//48/207), and the latter achieves some intimacy (of whose degree we can never be sure) with Pozdnyshev's wife through his ability to play music with her. Music has a vital role in the possible seduction of Pozdnyshev's wife resembling that played by the romance tale in Dante's account of the illicit love of Paolo and Francesca in Canto V of *Inferno*. Like Dante, the accent here is on art as a means of seduction, as a kind of beauty that has as much power to corrupt as it has to save; and the romance is a corrupting art just as, presumably, the sonata by Beethoven from which the story takes its name.

The choice of music is not accidental. Nor is the choice of Beethoven, the quintessentially romantic composer. During the romantic period, and in its wake, music assumed an exalted status, as the most authentically universal form of art.[17] Music's availability to widely different audiences, its capacity to affect them in ways that are hard if not impossible to articulate, contributed to its newly found authority. Music becomes the voice of being, of that plenitude from which, as I noted in my comments on *War and Peace* and *Anna Karenina*, we are otherwise perpetually alienated. Music binds all together in this sense. But it also loosens in binding, throwing off all rational restraint: if music brings us together, it does so at the cost of our individuality, of the forms of intelligibility that allow us to negotiate our way in the world. Music demands we surrender ourselves. Now, surrender is not necessarily negative, but the moralist may object that it is so to the degree it fosters unbridled sensuality.

Pozdnyshev is nothing if not consistent, and his condemnatory view of music is a case in point. Music, as the most universal of the arts, is also the most dangerous, the one most likely to sweep away the restraints of morality, no matter how false they may be. Hence, the appearance of the musically inclined Trukhachevsky terrifies Pozdnyshev; his ensuing nightmare of jealous suspicion feeds on this view. But, what is more, in sweeping away the restraints of morality, music shows the truth, yet another unbearable truth, that morality is merely a fragile construction, a pusillanimous attempt to direct the violent energies of the animal to ends that are not wholly destructive. By killing his wife, Pozdnyshev recognizes this truth and expresses his inability to tolerate it. Pozdnyshev does not want to accept that the animal rules in us even though his entire "confession" is directed to that end. The murder is ambiguous in this respect. While it is no doubt an act of animal brutality, a quick reaction, the fact that it is motivated by a complicated jealousy indicates just how impurely animal this brutality is. For jealousy might be the animal desire to secure a mate, but it also might be a symptom of a creature tormented by its own frailty, its own animality. Both elements seem to be at work in Pozdnyshev's confession, and they go to show the painful tenuousness of a finite creature caught between attachment to and rejection of its own limitations, and the order of nature that imposes them.

Against Plato

From this perspective, the tormented desire for sex is the model for all desire, which is inherently tyrannical and selfish. The inevitable result of pursuing, not extirpating desire, is the murder of others, whether literal or figurative, a point also made by Dostoevsky. While the concern about the nature of desire is ancient, the solution is radically modern: it is the very essence of radicality since it demands that the species exterminate itself. Here the story is mad, and this madness both recalls and corrects Plato, whose *Symposium*, the supreme dialogue on the taming of desire, is also, strictly speaking, the recollection of a madman.[18]

The *Symposium* crucially redefines desire to suggest that it has both a physical and a metaphysical or spiritual aspect, that there is a base desire for material satisfaction and a more noble desire that is noble precisely because it cannot be satisfied.[19] Noble desire sees beyond shimmering, variable appearances to an ideal, immutable reality, the contemplation of which lifts us out of our miserable entrapment in the body, in the ever changing world of time and space. The Platonic gamble is that brute material desire may be tamed by transforming it into the more noble, subtle desire for the ideal that can never be realized, never brought to fleshly form without loss. This ideal became the Christian ideal that involves communion with God, the *unio mystica* [ecstatic union], with that which is not subject to coming into being or passing away—in a word, with that which is immortal.

Pozdnyshev rejects this thinking. He maintains that desire cannot be tamed, that to do so is merely to court a fiction, perhaps even a necessary one. If desire cannot be tamed, if it is not subordinate, then one is compelled to admit that it is base material desire and nothing else that rules in human life. And, if that is so, the kind of desperate mendacity exposed so well in both *The Death of Ivan Ilyich* and *The Kreutzer Sonata* is inevitable: it is of the very fabric of society itself. There is no purer state, no better society. We are trapped in lies we can neither do without nor tolerate, an evil that begets evil.

EVIL

"How Much Land Does a Man Need?" develops this notion of evil as born both of nature's hostility to human aspiration *and* of the human response to that hostility, the attempt to overcome our natural state that is the most radical form of rebellion against nature. This rebellion is richly and brutally ironic in so far as it signals a revolution of destruction: in trying to overcome nature, humanity destroys itself just as Pakhom, the Tolstoyan everyman, dies after having achieved his purpose. In this respect, "How Much Land Does a Man Need?" has paradigmatic quality; it is an austere *summa* of the dilemma that preoccupies the late works, perhaps all of Tolstoy's fiction.

"How Much Land Does a Man Need?" deals with the stuff of wisdom literature, and it is no surprise that Tolstoy exploits the parable form. In doing so, Tolstoy aligns himself with the ancients and their extreme concern to curb human desire. A crucial seam of ancient thought is captured beautifully in one of Tacitus' most evocative *sententiae*; namely, that the "desire to rule enflames the heart more than do all other passions."[20] Here Tacitus employs the comparative (*flagrantior*: literally "more aflame") to suggest that desire burns up the one who is driven to rule, to dominate, and, of course, this is precisely the point that the parable seems to make.

Now, one may argue that the parable is simply advancing commonplaces of the tradition in a new garb, dressing up the warnings that have accompanied all portrayals of great men, and thereby also renewing the famous attack on the essentially pagan notion of the great man that reemerged in the modern era with Napoleon. While there is truth to this argument, I think it undervalues the most interesting aspect of the parable's portrayal of desire, its pronounced circularity. If Pakhom is first enflamed by desire in a curiously playful reference to the temptation of Adam, his attempts to achieve satisfaction take on a circular pattern that becomes an emblem, an epigrammatically reductive narrative extending to all human striving that is Sisyphean and, as such, suggests that the essential desire to overcome necessary limitation—and necessity itself—is one that can only be satisfied in death: as long as there is life there is futility and the cruelest evil of all, the impossibility of freedom from interest, of release from the conditions of corporeal enslavement.

I should like to address these points in more detail first by taking a careful look at the notion of property, the object of Pakhom's desire, as a metaphor for this sort of freedom, and then turning to discuss the narrative structure that Pakhom's desire creates in the main body of the parable.

Land Ownership as Metaphor

Tolstoy came to view property ownership as a kind of violence. He thereby recognized the assumptions inherent in the declaration that some thing is mine, subject to my exclusive use and benefit. While one may well trace the origin of this particular view to the influence of Proudhon, whose famous aphorism, "Property is theft," has the virtue of simplicity, it has strong precedents in Christian tradition and specifically literary precedents within the Russian context as well. The most notable among the latter is perhaps the horse-whipping scene in Dostoevsky's *Crime and Punishment* where the brutal peasant, Mikolka, claims to justify his right to beat his horse to death because the horse is his property and, thus, he has the power to dispose of it as he sees fit. If it is crucial to note that in Mikolka's case the property is animate and not a mere object, both the essentially coercive nature of ownership and the monstrous power it seems to grant a human being are represented with unforgettable clarity.

For what is ownership but the pretense to obtain permanent possession of some thing, as if possession transcended the vicissitudes of time, the ceaseless pattern of generation, and decay that remains our master? Rousseau suggests that ownership is the root of evil, the hardly innocent expression for the imposition of law on nature, of human desire on that which may seem forever frightfully distant from it. If I own some thing, I assert my indefinite and unrestricted control over it, my godlike dominion to dispose of that property as I see fit without any restriction whatsoever. Ownership is the assertion that nature can be brought to heel, can be made to our specifications, and that, in so doing, human beings demonstrate their essential power to determine their fate rather than having it determined for them.

To assert ownership and thereby deny the true state of affairs is to rebel against nature, to make it something that is recognizably human.

But the price of ownership in this sense is illusion, the fact that nature cannot be itself if it is to be some thing for us. This is a way of expressing Kant's crucial point that the world is qualitatively divided between appearances and the origins they disguise.[21] Since human beings can only come to understand the world through mediations defining how the world appears to us, this being a sign of our radical dependency, the world as it is outside of these mediations in itself is utterly unknowable. As mediating beings we must destroy that world in the process of making it into "our" world. Alexandre Kojève, the influential Russo-French philosopher writes in his *Introduction to the Reading of Hegel*:

> In contrast to the knowledge that keeps man in a passive quietude, Desire dis-quiets him and moves him to action. Born of Desire, action tends to satisfy it, and can do so only by the "negation," the destruction, or at least the transformation, of the desired object: to satisfy hunger, for example, the food must be destroyed or, in any case, transformed. Thus, all action is "negating." Far from leaving the given as it is, action destroys it; if not in its being, at least in its given form. And all "negating-negativity" with respect to the given is necessarily active. But negating action is not purely destructive, for if action destroys an objective reality, for the sake of satisfying the Desire from which it is born, it creates in its place, in and by that very destruction, a subjective reality. The being that eats, for example, creates and preserves its own reality by over-coming a reality other than its own, by the "transformation" of an alien reality into its own reality, by the "assimilation," the "inter-nalization" of a "foreign," "external" reality.[22]

And here is the deepest sense of the notion of ownership, the capacity to make the world in our own image, and this means the capacity to make the world in accordance with our desires, a virtual product of desire. The world has worth only in so far as it can be brought within the purview of human domination. The obvious con-nection between property and empire comes into its own in this context where the greatest imperialism is reflected in the desire to become master of the human estate in every manner possible, that of history's Napoleons, Newtons, Spinozas and, indeed, of the great, holistic writers, like Tolstoy himself. Of course the ominous aspect of this essentially imperialistic urge is that it is inherently destructive of the "raw" materials that it first encounters and seeks to overcome. Nature becomes a thing only as a result of human manipulation, its being is attached once and forever to its utility for us.

If ownership is the object of desire, the essence of desire is movement toward this object, a movement that expresses itself as a narrative. All narratives are histories of desire, the striving to achieve some end. The question that lies nestled within the circular narrative structure of Tolstoy's parable addresses this paradoxical aspect of narrative: the narrative quest for an end to all narrative, a quest that destroys its object in the attempt to possess it.

Narrative against Itself

The very heart of the parable is conflict, the struggle to possess what cannot be possessed, either by Pakhom's desperate measures or by the narrative that "contains" them itself. There is an overlap between tale and teller that does not permit for a satisfactory resolution. Pakhom dies, and the narrative ends in a quiet declaration of the irrelevance of narrative: each new beginning is merely a repetition of the old pattern until he reaches the final escape, death. Let me examine how this comes to pass.

The parable begins innocently enough with an amusing play on the story of the fall contained in Genesis. The two sisters engage in a contest over whose life is better, that of the merchant in town or that of the peasant in the countryside. The entire exchange between the sisters turns on the question of material benefit and whether seeking greater material benefit is worth the risk. The contrast between these two kinds of life is a familiar one in Tolstoy's writings. The city is a profound manifestation of the desire to overcome nature, to extract oneself from it, and thereby to wrap oneself in the illusion that nature can be overcome—for what is a city if not the product of human will, the substitution of a man-made environment for an ostensibly natural one? It is thus transparently significant that the initial temptation in the parable comes from a comparison of different kinds of lives, one that seeks to overcome nature and one that abides by it. The promise of material well-being, of prosperity and risk, raises this issue, and it is a typical irony of the parable that Pakhom, while praising his wife's spirited defense of peasant unease concerning the material pursuits that dominate city life, makes his fatal declaration that "given as much land as he could wish for, he would fear no one, not even the devil himself" (25:I//68/97). Here the desire for as much land as one could wish for (*"bud' zemli vvoliu"*) is the one expression of desire that initiates the pattern dominating the remainder of the parable; to use traditional, Christian imagery, this temptation is the spark that incinerates Pakhom's life itself. Tolstoy invokes this Christian reading with his reference to the devil at the end of the first chapter. This reference emphasizes the folktale aspect of the narrative, the traditional equation of desire with the forces of evil.

The narrative thus initially places itself within a traditional pattern of temptation and fall. But this narrative differs from that of the *felix culpa*, the so-called "fortunate fall," where temptation and fall are essential elements in learning, in a progression toward the truth. Instead, Pakhom's repeated attempts to reestablish a state of blissful calm describe unceasing struggle toward an end that vanishes in the moment of being possessed. Here the apparently ruthless honesty of the narrative is its refusal to tame desire, to suggest that desire can be the engine of progress, of movement from a state of ignorance to enlightenment. To the contrary, the parable takes a typically darker view of desire: if the narrative of the fortunate fall translates momentary error into lasting benefit, a narrative that admits of no such improvement affirms the continuous repetition of the same, a vain purposiveness.

In Tolstoy's parable, this repetition is made only more violent by the increase in the extremity of Pakhom's desire each time he acquires a new piece of property. The more he acquires, the more he wants to acquire: to educate desire does not bring it under control but only increases its intensity. This increase is of considerable interest because it reveals that Pakhom's desire is for unconditional control over the land, a possession that admits of no challenges from others and, ultimately, from time itself (after all, Pakhom seeks land that he can possess "for ever," *v vechnost'*). The notion of temptation in the parable is a good deal more subtle than it might seem at first blush. The lust for acquisition turns out to be a lust for freedom, a powerful underlying desire to be rid of limitation on unbridled exercise of one's will.

This very important point comes to the fore as the goad that compels Pakhom to seek out more property. His first property acquisition after the opening temptation scene involves some land that he purchases from a local landowner. He decides to make this purchase because he is harassed by the landowner's estate manager who constantly imposes fines on the peasants if their animals stray onto the landowner's property. Pakhom wants freedom from this kind of harassment, and here the notion of property ownership is associated with a striving for freedom from the dominion of others.

The motif gains momentum with the next acquisition. This time Pakhom is harassed not by the estate manager of the landowner but by other peasants whose animals stray onto his new property. The obvious irony of this circumstance notwithstanding, the essence of the problem is limitation, the fact that Pakhom is unable to enjoy his property without interference, that his power is not supreme. This fuels the desire to obtain more property that will lead him to travel to the rather far away lands of the Bashkirs.

This final act of acquisition is of course the fulcrum of the entire parable. What tempts Pakhom is the chance to acquire a huge tract of land, to escape once and for all from the restrictions placed on his ownership of land in the previous instances, to possess unconditionally. It is thus rather apt that Pakhom chooses to seek his fortune among a different people because he is in effect turning his back on society, on the restrictions to individual desire that form the core sacrifice of freedom necessary for the creation of civil order.

Pakhom's attempt to obtain a virtually unconditional power fails, and it fails because the very terms by which he tries to obtain the unattainable undermine his desire. Pakhom's acquisition of land is restricted by his inability to cover an unlimited amount of space within a limited time. In the space of a day, as the sun shines, Pakhom must try to cover as much ground as he can—in other words, Pakhom's quest for land can be wheeled out as a transparent allegory of life itself, this brief time that human beings have in the sun, where they seek to maximize their power before the sun goes down. Pakhom completes his task and dies, a fitting conclusion to his journey and a coda to desire for the unconditional, the expression of evil, which strives to terminate itself in satisfaction.

There is nothing new in this. If we look back on the territory we have covered in the preceding stories, the evidence is overwhelming: in them the accusation of desire's perfidy announced in *Anna Karenina* has become dogmatic, obsessive, repetitive. All the stories maintain that we must have narratives to overcome nature's hostility, the fundamental conditions imposed on us as living beings by an indifferent nature. But they also maintain that such narratives are screens, forms of deception, at once indispensable and intolerable inducements to life. They are evil, serving the lie, making promises they cannot keep. And this is a point of cutting irony when one considers that it is Tolstoy's narratives themselves that successfully inform us of the perfidiousness of narrative. If narratives are a mendacious art of forgetting, they can also unmask themselves as such, emancipating us from the illusions they create.

But what kind of emancipation is this? Are there no narratives driven by those who have emancipated themselves from the illusions of desire, who have relinquished the need to create lies in order to live? Are there no positive narratives of relinquishment? Is relinquishment outside narrative?

INEQUALITY

To offer an answer to these questions, let us examine one late work, *Master and Man*, that seems to be a narrative of successful relinquishment, a narrative that abandons conditionality, the necessary inequality created by our physical limitation in favor of the equality that is the highest attribute of relinquishment. In doing so, *Master and Man* returns us to the problem of the labyrinth with which we began our exploration of Tolstoy's fiction many pages ago, revealing an intriguingly positive aspect of the infinite, that it fosters equality, dissolving hierarchy like a snow storm, the narrative's central metaphor.

The story begins with a typically blunt contrast between a character who seeks to bend fate to his will and one who is resigned to fate. This contrast echoes the fundamental tension in *War and Peace* between the striving for mastery and relinquishment of such striving. The merchant, Vassily Brekhunov, is the small-town Napoleon and his servant Nikita is yet another avatar of Karataev. But, as avatar, he is hardly the same as Karataev; nor is he pristinely virtuous. He is a drunkard, after all.

The plot of the story is simple. Brekhunov wants to buy a wood lot and is afraid that, if he tarries, he will not be able to do so at an advantageous price. As a result, he wants to settle the deal as quickly as possible and has to travel to the village where the seller lives. The weather is not favorable—it is high winter—and his wife asks him to take the servant Nikita along just in case. The journey is disastrous, resulting in Brekhunov's death. Both he and Nikita move in circles as they try to arrive at the seller's town in increasingly bad weather. They are foiled by the storming snow that levels everything, eliminating all markers by which the two can navigate. They lose their way.

Brekhunov, who foolishly insisted on going ahead despite the storm, gives his life for Nikita who is the only one to survive.

There is particular irony here, since Brekhunov has nothing obviously heroic about him: he is venal, ruthless and vain, the heroic image reduced to its ugliest basic elements. For what else is the ancient hero, the seeker after glory, than the promotion of self-glorification against all others? What exalts the ancient, pagan hero, and gives him some similarity to the Christian hero who emerges in his wake, is the marked absence of the fear of death. Or, if there is fear, the pagan hero overcomes it; this is the root of his heroic nature. What distinguishes the pagan from the Christian hero is, however, precisely the attitude to glory or the kind of glory each seeks. The pagan hero seeks glory as immortality, as the most unrestrained variety of self-aggrandizement. The Christian hero does not seek such glory, but glorious humility, the subordination of the individual, the "self" to others; the Christian hero submits, his immortality expresses a freedom from the selfish cares of the body.

Brekhunov is remarkable because he discards his decadent, modern ideal of ancient glory, the bourgeois pursuit of enrichment, to become a Christian hero. In this respect, his transformation or conversion at the very end of the story is of abiding interest. The key question here concerns Brekhunov's motives: why does he change so quickly? Typical conversion accounts, from Paul through Augustine, point to the intervention of a mysterious or miraculous authority or to an outstanding secularization thereof like that created by Dickens in "A Christmas Carol."[23] But in *Master and Man* there is none of this, only a paragraph more remarkable for what it omits:

> Vasily Andreyich stood in silence, without moving, for half a minute and then suddenly, with the same decisiveness with which he shook hands over a good bargain, took a step back, pushed up his sleeves, and with both hands started shoveling the snow off Nikita and out of the sledge. When he'd shifted it all, he hastily undid his belt, opened his fur coat wide, and, pushing Nikita down, lay on top of him, covering him not only with his fur coat but his own glowing, overheated body. Pushing down the laps of his overcoat between the sledge sides and Nikita with his hands, and pinning the hem down with his knees, Vasily Andreyich, lay prone, leaning his head on the front of the sledge. Now he heard neither the horse's movements, nor the howling wind, attending

only to Nikita's breathing. At first Nikita lay motionless for a long time. Then he breathed in noisily and stirred. (29:IX//41–2/106)

This paragraph gives no reason for the sudden change in Brekhunov's attitude. The most plausible inference might locate the change in Brekhunov's attempt to escape the trap in which he and Nikita find themselves. For Brekhunov rides Mukhorty with the urgency of a man used to acting and not to waiting passively to die. This is his desperate move, a final expression of the will to take hold of things, to wrest advantage from fate. The failure of this escape might support an inference that Brekhunov's change in attitude is due to a sober realization of the extremity and hopelessness of his situation. Terrified by this realization, Brekhunov turns to sacrifice himself, a sort of suicide. One can easily imagine the allegorical riches to be mined here. Brekhunov in the face of death, nature's snowy indifference, nobly sacrifices himself, becoming truly Christian by recognizing the vanity of selfish striving, the evanescence of material joys in comparison with the immortal joy to be gained from submission to the other, an *imitatio Christi*.

While there is no reason to diminish these kinds of readings, they fail to answer the question "Why?" There is considerable cunning in this odd circumstance. What does it mean here, after all, to answer the question "Why?" Any answer would have to be the result either of supernatural intervention—revelation—or rational calculation. Since both are absent from this paragraph, one is left to pursue the other main alternative: that there is no answer, no reason why. Brekhunov's decision is necessarily enigmatic, it features a turning away from the networks of understanding that have guided his life (and, presumably, those of the reader as well). There is, then, an ineradicably aleatory quality to Brekhunov's decision that is the necessary result of abjuring these networks: his is a truly free, immortal act.

This way of viewing Brekhunov's change of heart no doubt sits poorly with those who seek an authority that reveals itself at a moment of crisis. But it is a singularly astute presentation of the purest conversion, the becoming utterly "other" that is self-sacrifice; for self-sacrifice must reflect a disinterest in self that simply eliminates the vitiating conditions of physical existence reflected in motives or reasons why. Brekhunov's is the beautifully free act whose beauty stems from the extremity of its escape from the world of interest, of the recalcitrant body. Moreover, through this act Brekhunov achieves a freedom from self that allows him to perceive his underlying equality with Nikita.

The narrative insinuates that this is the essence of equality, that it is predicated on freedom from interest, from the kind of desire that directed Brekhunov, and which we have encountered in Tolstoy's deluded masters who strive to exalt themselves above all others.

Equality thus demands the relinquishment of interest. But can the latter be lastingly achieved by one who consciously returns to it? Can one consciously pursue equality? The story is silent about these questions. Brekhunov's death allows it to be so. If we think back on the many characters who have tried to relinquish disquieting desire, the examples of Pierre Bezukhov and Levin stand out as hinting, rather darkly, that this return may well be impossible. But this hint is only fitting, since return to equality is a striving to empty oneself of what one is, to become nothing, to be exempted from the interests of the world. This state is most akin to death, one impossible to square with lived life. In this sense, equality takes us back, at the very end of our journey through Tolstoy's fiction, to that nothingness which Olenin discovers in the stag's lair, to the labyrinthine center without a center that holds Tolstoyan narrative together just as it threatens to pull it apart.

The narrative of relinquishment confirms that relinquishment can have no narrative. One must search elsewhere for that final point which presents the living truth of all things, that gets us there without killing us, literally and figuratively.

CHAPTER 4

A PROPHET?

JUSTIFICATION OF THE WORLD

A Confession, the inaugural work of Tolstoy's Christian militancy, is a good place to start exploration of his attempt to create a living revelation of truth overcoming the inscrutable perplexity of our being in the world. The fount of that perplexity, death, which shreds the aspirations of the body just as its spectral shadow, the infinite, shreds those of the mind, thus forms the primary subject matter of the work, which seeks to offer a *cosmodicy* or *theodicy*: a justification of the world. While this overriding concern with death and the infinite evinces a commonality of theme that links *A Confession* to Tolstoy's earlier fiction, the radical difference lies in the treatment of these themes, in Tolstoy's attempt to fashion a new rhetoric adequate to the task of promoting a Christian doctrine—a revealed teaching—that utterly rejects the aporetic ambiguity of his greatest fictional works.

The title of *A Confession* heralds the new tone, alluding to its immensely prestigious predecessors by St Augustine and Jean-Jacques Rousseau, the former being a spiritual, the latter an ostensibly secular autobiography. While Tolstoy's work shares important traits with these predecessors, prominent among which are Augustine's pathos of conversion, the unblemished self-representation of Rousseau, and the rhetorical virtuosity characteristic of both, *A Confession* is also strikingly original: its dogged focus on death and the infinite as well as its ecumenical use of imagery and anecdote have no exact parallel in either of its predecessors. Moreover, *A Confession* is a work of demanding concision and concentration, a brevity that seeks to say in a paragraph what entire books are unable to say.

Nevertheless the work begins conventionally enough with a tale of corruption and disillusionment, yet another Tolstoyan indictment of society, which allows its members to look away from the fundamental questions of life. As we have seen already, Tolstoy is inherently suspicious of the accepted ways of society—its traditions—since he infers that these ways are accepted because they liberate individuals from thought and responsibility for their actions. In Erich Heller's words: "Tradition is the wise agreement not to ask certain questions, to narrow the domain of the questionable, and grant the mind a firm foundation of answers which can be taken for granted" (14). Heller's reference to "wisdom" here is quite ironic; it assumes that the attainment of wisdom is a blissful freedom from thought, a return to animal innocence and immortality.

Tolstoy counters that this state can only be achieved at the cost of moral inertia. And it is remarkable, if wholly consistent, that his witnessing an execution (in Paris in 1857) stirs him from acceptance of his society and the exculpatory pieties that justify it:

> When I saw how the head was severed from the body and heard the thud of each part as it fell into the box, I understood not with my intellect but with my whole being, that no theories of the rationality of existence or of progress could justify such an act; I realized that even if all the people in the world from the day of creation found this to be necessary according to whatever theory, I knew that it was not necessary and that it was wrong. (23: III//8/23)

Tolstoy then refers to the death of his brother: "He suffered for over a year and died an agonizing death without ever understanding why he lived and understanding even less why he was dying. No theories could provide any answers to these questions, either for him or for me, during his slow and painful death" (23:III//8/23). While Tolstoy indicates that he managed to silence the fundamental questions about the world posed by these two deaths, it is quite evident that death keeps its hold on him as what cannot fit into any rational order of life. The combination of an execution with a "natural" death underscores the connection of death with evil. If we were not subject to death, evil, the negation of life, would not have its shadowy, perplexing "in-existence."[1] Why bring up evil here? Tolstoy's juxtaposition of an execution with the death of his brother is artful, cunning: it is a sardonic way of looking at the human as the *imago Dei*, the image of God. For the latter is the great executioner, and Tolstoy asks how there can be any rational justification for death so understood. Tolstoy, just like St Augustine, poses the question of evil, the question that arises from the discord between the attribution of benevolence to God, or of rationality to the working of the world (the philosophers' version of benevolence), and the fact of death, of limitation, of defeat that haunts every human life. What can be benevolent about an ordering of things that denies us our greatest, most intimate wish: to be free and, above all, to be free of death?

"Whence evil, whence death?"—this is the great question, the defining question of *A Confession*. The brilliance of *A Confession* is to pose this question with a brute clarity and focus that avoids the tendency to obfuscation, to a sort of inventive turning away that is the eternal temptation at the heart of literature, philosophy, and religion, of all attempts to make us at home in our mortality. Tolstoy's vaunted tendency to estrangement is no more powerfully at work than in *A Confession*, which seeks to estrange us from any comfort, any means devised to staunch the ebbing away of our life.

While this conclusion seems to be justified by the initial part of *A Confession*, Tolstoy cannot leave it at that: he must find the "happy ending," the way of enduring death, and he finds only faith capable of aiding him. Indeed, the "plot" of *A Confession* is much less interesting than the way in which it is enacted. The plot is a simple description of error on the way to truth, of human waywardness that can and must be corrected. The very same writing that sets out with icy mastery the broadest question pertaining to human existence moves to answer it with shocking precipitancy. The god and man in Tolstoy cannot find respite from their continual combat.

What do I mean by this? After setting out the question, Tolstoy moves to condemn certain responses to it, those of art and reason, of literature and philosophy. Tolstoy makes very short work of literature as vanity, as a deluded way to immortality:

"Art, literature . . . ?" Under the influence of success and praise from others I had persuaded myself for a long time that this was something that may be done in spite of the approaching death that will annihilate everything—myself, my works, and the memory of them. But I soon saw that this, too, was delusion. It became clear to me that art is an ornamentation of life, something that lures us into life. (23:IV//14/32)

Following a long tradition, Tolstoy likens art and literature to something sweet that turns our gaze away from death. Here Tolstoy merely gives voice to a point of view everywhere present in his literary works, one of whose most astonishing qualities is the combination of fervent artistic mastery with an utter disrespect for that mastery, an art that so distrusts itself that it anticipates the terminal experiments of the twentieth century. This formidable, manifold irony is a fatal flaw for the author of *A Confession* who seeks to rid himself of dissimulation, the attachment to illusion that is the lifeblood of irony.

If art is an equivocal stimulant, reason is inherently hostile to life. This, at least, seems to be the guiding thread of the argument against reason that constitutes one of the centerpieces of the text. This argument is not against reason as a subservient structure of thought, but against reason as an independent, sovereign way of grasping the world. The argument against reason's sovereignty should be quite familiar by now: it impugns reason's capacity to grasp the whole because the whole is inscrutably infinite. The operative contrast is again between the discursive quality of human thinking, its dependence on mediations of various kinds, and the seamless, timeless quality of the whole, which can never be understood by some form of division into units or parts—the barest requirement of discursive thought—but only as it is in itself, in its seamless plenitude. The fact that it is only through the operation of reason that we can conceive of reason's limits serves merely to bolster the argument, to demonstrate the frailty of reason that, like all human things, sees itself most clearly by reference to its limitations. The whole can only be conceived as what is unavailable to thought. The infinite is the mirror in which reason sees both itself and what it cannot see.

Despite our familiarity with the matter, let us take a brief look at Tolstoy's argument, which starts with a decisive assumption: the only knowledge having any purchase on authority is absolute knowledge, a kind of knowledge so complete that it rules out any possibility of error. Tolstoy focuses on a particular example, the supposed law of development, which one can glean from empirical observation. He writes:

> Everything is developing and being differentiated, becoming more complex and moving toward perfection, and there are laws governing this process. You are part of the whole. If you learn as much as possible about the whole and if you learn the law of its

development, you will come to know your place in the whole and to know yourself. (23:V//17/35)

But he recognizes that this project is doomed to failure, and his reasons are telling:

As I examined the nature of this law more closely, it became clear to me that there could be no such law of eternal development. It became clear to me that to say everything is developing, becoming more perfect, growing more complex and being differentiated in endless space and time amounted to saying nothing at all. None of these words has any meaning, for in the infinite there is nothing either simple or complex, nothing before or after, nothing better or worse. (23:V//17–18/36)

The infinite assures the impossibility of discovering one's place in the whole. The infinite assures, thus, that no one can ascertain the reason for his or her existence. This is to say that there is no reason for existence, that existence and rationality are separated by an unbridgeable gulf. Such an assertion confirms what Tolstoy's great fictional works impress upon our imagination: all the ways by which we seek to find our place in the whole, whether driven by a desire to master our destiny or merely to determine what it might be, are forms of bare self-assertion. There is no hope of uncovering a divine pattern; and, indeed, there may be no such pattern. Reason leads to impasse. The only way of passing beyond that impasse is an arbitrary decision, an act of will that cannot justify itself other than through a lie. "I could not be deceived. All is vanity. Happy is he who has never been born; death is better than life; we must rid ourselves of life" (23: VI//27/49).

But *A Confession* does not of course end there. Some force impels Tolstoy further, and he refers to it as a "consciousness of life" (23: VIII//31/55). Here, ten years later, is the conceptual armature of *War and Peace*. But there is a certain, perhaps predictable change of emphasis to the extent that reason's frailty, its utter dependence on this consciousness of life, is even more pronounced. To put this in different terms, the conflict between reason and revelation that lies under the speculative framework of *War and Peace* is even more explicitly addressed in *A Confession*—perhaps it first comes to be grasped as the fundamental problem in the latter text. Yet, the outcome is sealed in advance, since reason cannot compete with revelation. In a move that is formally similar to, but in content strikingly at variance with, the thinking of his most radical European contemporaries, Tolstoy claims that revelation is the ground of reason, that there can be no independent rationality. All rationality is determined by a prior revelation, which, itself, cannot be subject to rational critique.

The consequences of this return to an essentially theocratic vision of the world are very disturbing. They flow from the problematic character of revelation. If all processes of reasoning depend for their content (and, ultimately, for their form as well) on a prior revelation, then, strictly speaking, there is no common ground from which to argue among different types of revelation. All revelation is privileged. The enormous effort of modern rationality to provide that common ground simply dissolves, inviting not discussion but conflict. If disputes cannot be solved by reason, then the alternative is obvious: only violent refutation is conclusive. Nonetheless, Tolstoy seems to stake all on revelation, holding that reason has authority only when subservient to revelation and, even then, this authority is derived, secondary. The assumption guiding Tolstoy here is the same one that guides all who see in revelation the only authority: revelation always says the same thing. No matter what the historical or cultural circumstances, the truths which govern are the same, if seen through a slightly different lens in each case. This elementary error, which just assumes the commonality in question, fosters the illusion that there is something seen in common prior to the particular seeing which that different lens first makes possible, an obvious contradiction that begs the question or simply poses it again.

But *A Confession* offers a far more problematic variant of this dilemma, one that withdraws the certainty of revelation, of its authority over reason. In a remarkable paragraph Tolstoy writes:

> Thus I turned to a study of the very theology that at one time I had completely rejected as unnecessary. Then it had struck me as so much useless nonsense; then I had been surrounded by life's phenomena, which I thought to be clear and full of meaning. Now I would have been glad to free myself of everything that did not foster a healthy mind, but I did not know how to escape. Rooted in this religious teaching, or at least directly connected to it, is the one meaning of life that has been revealed to me. No matter how outrageous it might seem to me in my old stubborn intellect, here

lies the one hope of salvation. It must be examined carefully and attentively in order to be understood, even if I do not understand it in the way I understand the position of science. I do not and cannot seek such an understanding of it due to the peculiar nature of the knowledge of faith. I shall not seek an explanation of all things. I know that the explanation of all things, like the origin of all things, must remain hidden in infinity. But I do not want to understand in order that I might be brought to the inevitably incomprehensible; I want all that is incomprehensible to be such not because the demands of the intellect are not sound (they are sound, and apart from them I understand nothing) but because I perceive the limits of the intellect. I want to understand, so that any instance of the incomprehensible occurs as a necessity of reason and not as an obligation to believe. (23:XVI//56–7/90–1)

The final line hints at a much less servile role for reason, a rejection of the venerable *credo quia absurdum* [I believe because it is absurd]. Indeed, rather than belief grounding and prescribing the limits of reason, this line suggests quite the contrary: that belief finds its proper place as a *supplement* to reason, as a means to fill in gaps whose identity is prescribed by reason and not as an end (and beginning) in itself. Does this complication entail the primacy of reason over revelation, what might appear to bring with it a reversal of the position that Tolstoy had already set out in his text? The answer to this question cannot be affirmative, for Tolstoy has already taken pains to indicate how reason leads to aporias. But these aporias only emerge because reason cannot ground itself. What Tolstoy seems to be after is (once again) an intriguing, if intrinsically unstable, synthesis or reconciliation of reason and revelation that owes more to axiomatic thought, thus, to modern mathematics, than it does to Christian dogmatics. Tolstoy's manner of thinking is something like this: reason has limits, it cannot ground itself. Therefore reason, if it is to retain any legitimacy, must proceed from a given, a ground accepted as such, a pure postulate or axiom. Faith can provide the given, the axiomatic foundation, if purified of absurdities, of contradictions.

This position amounts to rational faith, as many critics have suggested,[2] and it is fraught with difficulties no less severe than those that arise from a faith purged of reason. For the threshold question—which of faith or reason retains the primary authority?—receives no definitive answer. While it perhaps seems at first glance that reason is authoritative because its limits determine where belief must fulfill its function, the mere fact that faith has to fulfill such a function tends in the opposite direction, toward the discrediting of reason. The end result is a negative union in which neither faith nor reason can retain authority without the other. While this union might appear to be an attractive one because it works a reconciliation of otherwise incompatible ways of grasping the world, its inherent instability cannot be eliminated. And it is undeniable that Tolstoy's later writings reveal important traces of this instability in so far as Tolstoy is never able fully to dedicate himself to one discourse to the exclusion of the others. He is neither a wholly convinced rationalist nor believer nor creator. Indeed, *A Confession* ends with a dream, a fiction, albeit an ideologically obedient one, that provides a neat figuration of Tolstoy's discovery of faith.[3]

The fruit of this negative union in the religious sphere is very telling. *A Confession*, which isolates the problem, was to be followed by a massive treatise on the revealed truth as expressed in the Gospels in which all impurities accumulated due both to theological and textological speculation would be sifted away to present the unalloyed universal core of Christian revelation. The treatise in turn was to be followed by Tolstoy's own profession of faith in *What I Believe*. These two doctrinal works, the former remaining unfinished at Tolstoy's death, develop the most characteristic approaches and principles of Tolstoy's faith; they evince, on all levels, the difficulties pertaining to Tolstoy's apparent resolution of the conflict between reason and revelation.

TOLSTOY'S NEW DOCTRINE

The immense, unfinished treatise has two main parts: a critique of Russian Orthodox theology and a careful translation and consolidation of the Gospels from the point of view announced in the critique. Tolstoy's critique is famous and of extraordinary radicality: he identifies a central problem in Christian dogma, a conflict between Christ's twin roles as lawgiver and redeemer, that cuts across all variants of Christian faith. The conflict may be expressed as follows: Why should Christ formulate a teaching, advocating a new way of living, for which redemption is nonetheless still necessary? This peculiar circumstance suggests that following the new teaching is not enough for one to be saved, that no matter how assiduous one is in fulfilling

Christ's teaching, one must have one's life redeemed. Law and grace cannot be reconciled: either one or the other must prevail. If that is not the case, no matter what one does, one will be in need of redemption. There is no salvation through Christ's teaching, there is no need for that teaching. Conversely, if the teaching were truly sufficient, there would be no need for redemption or salvation.

Tolstoy astutely saw that this conflict must take as its governing assumption the impossibility of realizing Christ's teaching on earth. For Tolstoy, there can be no other explanation why redemption could be relevant. Yet the governing assumption of the Tolstoyan revision of Christian dogma is just the opposite: there can be no sense to Christ's teaching other than that it *can* be realized on earth. If that were not so, Christ's teaching would be quite superfluous. The Christian life would be only a sort of cruel joke, a waiting for an inscrutable, divine decision since no matter what one does on earth, one remains outside the kingdom of heaven.

Tolstoy sees in this latter attitude not only a wretched perversion of logic, but a desire to enslave entirely at odds with Christ's message of liberation. From this perspective, Tolstoy's attack on the tortured logic of Christian dogma can be seen for what it is: a blistering condemnation of Christian metaphysics and otherwordliness as a means of legitimating a highly coercive, worldly authority, the church, by reference to its otherworldly origins. And, indeed, Tolstoy makes short work of the basic metaphysics grounding Christian doctrine. He discards the trinity as "nonsense"; he thereby eliminates all reference to the mixed nature of Christ as both God and man as well as to the privileged quality of the four Gospels as constituting the word of God. In proceeding thus Tolstoy relies on a venerable claim: that what is true withstands rational critique, for if a revealed truth is true, reason cannot find any way to dispute it successfully. Truth is truth. At the same time Tolstoy concedes that revelation may prevail only where reason finds its limits. But if reason can dispute revelation, it has not found its limits. In this respect, revelation becomes a supplement to reason, as noted above.

What emerges from this critique is a Gospel, purified of the accumulated sediment of interpretation favorable to the coercive practices of the church, that Tolstoy was savvy to produce in a condensed version, the so-called *Gospel in Brief*. This remarkable book, whose power the young Wittgenstein extolled while stationed on the Galician front in World War I, creates a new Christian teaching.[4]

Tolstoy summarizes the elements of that teaching with terse lucidity as follows:

1. Man is the son of an infinite source: a son of that father not by flesh but by the spirit.
2. Therefore man should serve the source in spirit.
3. The life of all men has a divine origin. It alone is holy.
4. Therefore man should serve that source in the life of all men. Such is the will of the Father.
5. The service of the will of that Father of life gives life.
6. Therefore the gratification of one's own will is not necessary for life.
7. Temporal life is the food for the true life.
8. Therefore the true life is independent of time: it is in the present.
9. Time is an illusion of life; life in the past and in the future conceals from men the true life of the present.
10. Therefore man should strive to destroy the illusion of the temporal life of the past and future.
11. True life is life in the present, common to all men and manifesting itself in love.
12. Therefore he who lives by love in the present, through the common life of all men, unites with the Father, the source and foundation of life. (24:802/118)

This is merely the abstract summary, however: the center of Tolstoy's revision of the Gospels, the fundamental positive teaching that emerges from this revision, is to be found elsewhere, in his powerful *profession de foi*, *What I Believe*.

The question here: What has the authority of accumulated dogma sought to suppress? What teaching of Christ's is most inimical to the constitution of authority? Tolstoy's answer: the prohibition against violence, the teaching of nonresistance to evil. The tremendous emphasis on this teaching as the "key that opens everything" (23:II//315/323) is the most distinctive aspect of Tolstoy's Christianity and the bulwark of his prophetic mission whose goal is nothing less than establishing the Kingdom of God on earth. Tolstoy puts the matter simply:

All my circumstances, my tranquility, the safety of myself and my family and my property were all based on a law repudiated by

Christ, on the law of a tooth for a tooth. The doctors of the Church taught that Christ's teaching was divine, but its performance impossible on account of human frailty, and only Christ's blessing can assist its performance. The worldly teachers and the whole construction of our life plainly admitted the impracticability and fantastic nature of Christ's teaching, and by words and deeds taught what was opposed to it. The admission of the impracticability of God's teaching had gradually to such a degree impregnated me and had become so familiar, and it coincided to such a degree with my desires, that I had never before noticed the contradiction with which I was faced. I did not see that it is impossible at one and the same time to confess Christ as God, the basis of whose teaching is non-resistance to him that is evil, and consciously and calmly to work for the establishment of property, law-courts, government, and military forces, to establish a life contrary to the teaching of Christ, and to pray to the same Christ that the law of non-resistance to him that is evil and of forgiveness should be fulfilled among us. (23:II//314–15/323–4)

The crucial point is to see that Tolstoy ascribes the basic significance of Christ's teaching (and, above all, his sacrifice) to its being a paradigmatic case both of nonresistance to evil and divine love. The claim he opposes, that only a God could make such a sacrifice, permits the establishment of authority through violence on earth and, as Tolstoy shows again and again, authority can establish itself on earth only through violence. Thus, the nonresistance to violence is the key gesture by which human hierarchies may be overturned, since all such hierarchies impose and thrive on violence: without violence they cannot be, and a totally new, hitherto impossible community must emerge.

Lest one think this is a new element in Tolstoy's thought, I should like to refer to Prince Andrei's fate in *War and Peace*, a fate that places the issue in admirably bold relief. After Prince Andrei is injured at Borodino, he is taken to a dressing station where he sees his erstwhile enemy, Anatole Kuragin. Rather than enmity, Prince Andrei feels an almost boundless sympathy for or, better, empathy with Anatole:

Prince Andrei could no longer restrain himself, and he wept tender, loving tears over people, over himself, and over their and his own errors.

"Compassion, love for our brothers, for those who love us, love for those who hate us, love for our enemies—yes, that love which God preached on earth, which Princess Marya taught me, and which I didn't understand; that's why I was sorry about life, that's what was still left for me, if I was to live. But now it's too late. I know it!" (11:III/2/XXXVII//258/904)

This feeling will be the kernel of what Prince Andrei later refers to as "divine love" as opposed to the earthly love that draws him to Natasha and to life again. The opposition, however, of earthly love and divine love makes the very point that Tolstoy seeks to emphasize in his critique of Christian dogma: that divine love, the way of the divine, cannot admit of realization on the earth. If no other argument militates for a change of perspective after the so-called conversion, this one certainly does, and it is an argument which offers a simple response to those who may believe it reveals but an esoteric posture (Gorky, for example), since that belief is supported by the very skepticism about the practicality of the Christian task which Tolstoy decries.

POLITICAL IMPLICATIONS

Tolstoy's interpretation of the Gospels and his insistence on the doctrine of nonresistance to evil as the cornerstone of Christ's teaching have extremely radical implications for the conduct of politics. I think it would be worthwhile here to examine some of these briefly, especially since a good part of Tolstoy's later activity was of a directly political nature.

The Kingdom of God Is Within You makes the political implications of Tolstoy's Christianity quite clear. Tolstoy writes:

Christianity in its true sense puts an end to government. So it was understood at its very commencement; it was for that cause that Christ was crucified. So it has always been understood by people who were not under the necessity of justifying a Christian government. Only from the time that the heads of government assumed an external and nominal Christianity, men began to invent all the impossible, cunningly devised theories by means of which Christianity can be reconciled with government. But no honest and serious-minded man of our day can help seeing the incompatibility of true Christianity—the doctrine of meekness, forgiveness of injuries, and love—with government, with pomp, acts of violence, executions, and wars. The profession of true Christianity not only excludes the possibility of recognizing government, but even destroys its very foundations. (28:X//186/236–7)

Tolstoy has been called an anarchist, but, even here, the term suffers from being loaded with exactly the kinds of assumptions Tolstoy is out to deny. Those who oppose anarchism usually do so based on the impracticality of anarchist thinking: Is it not true, after all, that without prohibitions, we will all rip each other apart, thus initiating that war of all against all that Hobbes considers to be our proper natural state? This kind of thinking makes its own assumptions, namely, that human beings are by nature evil, that they will commit heinous crimes in the absence of a punitive apparatus. But Tolstoy does not make this assumption: indeed, if there is any tacit assumption in Tolstoy's thinking here, it must be that human beings are not by nature evil. Rather, the refusal to accept that they may not be evil has ensured they will be so.

Tolstoy insists on the possibility that human beings are good, and that society has not allowed them to be so because society was created by a different imagination, the same kind of imagination that uses the fear of violent death as a reminder to obey. This imagination has nothing but contempt for human frailty, and, because it has so little faith in human beings, it seeks the most efficient means of enslaving them, whether through physical or more sophisticated modes of coercion.

In his *Concept of the Political* Carl Schmitt, the notorious German jurist and political philosopher, affirms this kind of thinking. He notes that the ". . . fundamental theological dogma of the evilness of the world and man leads, just as does the distinction of friend and enemy, to a categorization of men and makes impossible the undifferentiated optimism of a universal conception of man" (65). Conversely, Schmitt maintains that anarchism "reveals that the belief in the natural goodness of man is closely tied to the radical denial of state and government" (60). For Schmitt, anarchism is a naive refusal to engage in politics that seeks to eliminate the political entirely, to establish a new kind of hegemony, the reign of the universal. Is this what Tolstoy has in mind?

The answer to this question depends on how one defines the universal. A positive doctrine of the universal would have to delineate what that universal is, what kinds of universality can be appealed to in a positive manner as belonging to all human beings. But this notion of the universal entails many difficulties. Because it must assert identities, it necessarily excludes what does not align itself with those identities: exclusion points to the specter of violence, for every positive conceptual definition must subordinate its negation, and to do so is inherently violent. As Schelling notes: "the character of finitude is that nothing can be posited without at once positing its opposite" (1/70). Hence, even the positing of the universal as negative, as possessing no positive identity, implies the opposite because, in the mere act of positing, nothing becomes something, even if that "thing" is only definable as pure indeterminateness. The assumption or supposition that the universal is largely negative, a lack or privation of identity, in effect brings the concept of identity to its culmination in self-refutation.

Let me explain this carefully. If the identity that is given to the universal is wholly negative, then that identity resides in the privation of identity: identity is nonidentity, and the concept of identity cancels itself out. What remains is a universal negative: we are in so far as we are not; our finite identity drowns in the infinite. It is no coincidence that this concept of identity recalls or is an echo of Olenin's ecstatic experience in the stag's lair. The reconciliation of part and whole in a new universality is indeed a decision to embrace the negative, a *kenosis* or "emptying" whereby my identity surrenders itself completely.

This is why Tolstoy's insistence on this not being impossible is at once so important and so questionable. For is that not the crucial "sting" of embracing nonresistance to violence? I radically give up my self in so far as I am ready to allow it to be destroyed, to desist from self-assertion. Here the crucial move is already underway because I utterly negate myself in refusing to assert myself in the face of opposition. In order to attain universality, to create it among human beings, one must become nothing in this almost unqualified sense; the condition of freedom is a sort of termination of the self. The many avatars of Olenin, of which Brekhunov was last to be discussed, come to mind once again.

SALVAGING BELIEF?

While Tolstoy's "tracts" have often been considered the works of a cranky and wayward spirit, they in fact show an astute wager on the vital possibilities left in Christianity and on the best way to cultivate those possibilities. Tolstoy's key decision is to foreground Christ's teaching and to claim that it is realizable in this world; that, rather than setting an impossible task to human beings, a task whose impossibility will one day call forth a revolt against the entire system of belief, Christ seeks to create a new community with a new *ethos* [way of being]. As I have noted, the primary assumption in such a revaluation of this world is that human beings have the power to be good or are originally good, not being stained by some form of original sin that can only be redeemed through grace.

Living properly in this world involves an emptying of self, a decision in favor of living "by love in the present." Is this sort of sacrifice a radical *imitatio Christi* or a perfecting of Platon Karataev? Whatever the case may be, the continuity with central currents in the great novels is unmistakable along with the unfavorable status accorded not only to narrative but to thought as well. For to live in the present is to discard at once narrative and thought; at the very least, to live in the present is to denigrate them, to suggest that they are not germane to the blessed life.

The usual ironies abound. Tolstoy engages in a monumental destruction of the Christian tradition, an immense labor of exegesis and interpretation, to arrive at a doctrine that strives to be freed of both. And one wonders if this project of conscious forgetting can attain any more success than it did in the great novels. For only the needy, the too conscious, those who fear death as Tolstoy feared it, are likely to be seduced by the program he lays out. For the others, tradition should suffice.

Whatever its prospects for success, this project remains remarkable not only on account of its breathtaking audacity but for the way it anticipates one of the twentieth century's most notable tendencies: the striving to return to a point of beginning, of innocence, later despoiled by distorting sediments of commentary. One might refer here to various movements in art, like acmeism and futurism, or in philosophy, like phenomenology, that sought to return to the things themselves, to a simplicity of apprehension that would allow one to see again, refreshed and liberated.

CHAPTER 5

A PHILOSOPHER?

PHILOSOPHY AND RELIGION

Tolstoy's relation to philosophy requires some preliminary comment as to the nature of philosophy and its relation to faith. The confusion about this relation is endemic and problematic: within the Russian context, one frequently speaks of religious-philosophy as if that were an unproblematic combination. But, of course, it is hardly so and brings up several formidable questions about how philosophy in fact may be differentiated from faith. Heidegger puts the matter bluntly. He claims that philosophy must ask questions—philosophic questioning is the "piety of thinking"—and that, in this regard, philosophy and faith are radically different.[1] The philosopher questions everything, including the activity of philosophy itself (think of Pascal's "to philosophize is to engage in a mockery of philosophy"[2]), and this wide questioning is something that faith cannot engage in because it is a condition of faith's being what it is not to question its prime assumption: that God is. Heidegger famously writes, in regard to a basic question—"Why are there beings at all instead of nothing?":

> Now by referring to safety in faith as a special way of standing in the truth, we are not saying that citing the words of the Bible, "In the beginning God created heaven and earth, etc.," represents an answer to our question. Quite aside from whether this sentence of the Bible is true or untrue for faith, it can represent no answer at all to our question, because it has no relation to this question. It has no relation to it, because it simply cannot come into such a relation. What is really asked in our question is, for faith, foolishness.
> Philosophy consists in such foolishness. A "Christian philosophy" is a round square and a misunderstanding. To be sure, one

can thoughtfully question and work through the world of Christian experience—that is, the world of faith. That is then theology. Only ages that really no longer believe in the true greatness of the task of theology arrive at the pernicious opinion that, through a supposed refurbishment with the help of philosophy, a theology can be gained or even replaced, and can be made more palatable to the need of the age. Philosophy, for originally Christian faith, is foolishness. Philosophizing means asking: "Why are there beings at all instead of nothing?" Actually asking this means venturing to exhaust, to question thoroughly, the inexhaustible wealth of this question, by unveiling what it demands that we question. Whenever such a venture occurs, there is philosophy. (*Introduction to Metaphysics*, 8)

Heidegger maintains that the difference between philosophy and faith is that philosophy is interminably *zetic*, seeking, while faith is seeking only in a defined way, to confirm and elaborate its own grounding presupposition. Heidegger's definition of philosophy is admittedly radical: it is a return to the Socratic origins. There are many philosophers who would likely contest this view, but they, too, would balk at the notion of Christian philosophy. For philosophy differs from faith in the more fundamental way that it is the rational activity par excellence. Philosophy is the most comprehensive activity of reason, which both examines itself and the world; indeed, for the tradition that stems from Kant, these two kinds of examination are essentially one.

How, then, is Tolstoy a philosopher? Tolstoy is most authentically philosophical when he most seeks to negate the seductive multiplicity of experience in favor of identifying the unity behind it. In this sense, Tolstoy is most authentically philosophical when he is most nihilistic, most intent on getting behind appearances to the universal, infinite truth they conceal. No provocation is meant here; this is yet another way of describing the tension between perspective, the view of the moment, and that synoptic view of the whole we have previously encountered in Tolstoy's fiction, and particularly in *War and Peace*. For Tolstoy is always of two minds, both attached to and mistrustful of appearances. On the one hand, he is intensely this-worldly and practical: no other writer grasps the immersion in the things of the world better than Tolstoy. On the other hand, Tolstoy engages in what Slavoj Žižek calls the "elementary metaphysical gesture . . . the withdrawal from the immersion into a concrete life-world to the position of abstract observer."[3]

This abstract perspective—one that, strictly speaking, has no perspective—is the proper site of philosophy, which strives to grasp the whole through reason alone divorced of all the material restrictions and interests that impair that striving. Yet, Tolstoy's investigation reveals a remarkable affinity with Heidegger to the extent that, for Tolstoy, the closest reason can come to the whole, to an absolute, is through negation.

THE PHILOSOPHICAL "HEROES": ROUSSEAU AND SCHOPENHAUER

Tolstoy's engagement with philosophy was intense. Two philosophers in particular ignited his imagination: Jean-Jacques Rousseau and Arthur Schopenhauer.[4] This is a remarkable and telling combination, for both Rousseau and Schopenhauer elaborate sobering visions of human life, of entrapment and decline that dismiss the heady optimism often attributed—and superficially so—to the Enlightenment. While Schopenhauer's thought has been too frequently and easily dismissed as exemplary of an overweening pessimism (and, indeed, is there any other kind?), to place Rousseau in his company is perhaps a less customary move, although it can be amply justified. To explain why this is so, I shall present a necessarily sparse and schematic account of a basic pattern evident in both thinkers whose significance for Tolstoy should be readily apparent.

This pattern associates philosophical thinking with failure: in Rousseau's case, a failure to recover the inevitable loss of freedom, the greatest gift of our original state, which comes with the beginning of history.[5] In Schopenhauer's case, philosophical thinking, while identifying the falsity of human aspirations that are merely expressions of a blind and purposeless will, is unable to overcome them. Common to both is a poignant irony: philosophy recognizes the fundamental problems but cannot solve them. This latter responsibility belongs to art.

Rousseau

Rousseau is first and foremost a thinker of history and its relation to human freedom, our natural state. The state of nature is one of beatific innocence since, for Rousseau, it precedes time, the birth of consciousness and conscious—and that means reflective—reasoning. Rousseau maintains that human beings in their undifferentiated natural state partake of the immortality one may associate with animals; the chief index of that immortality is that animals do not know of their own death. He writes that "the knowledge of death and its terrors is one of man's first acquisitions in moving away from the animal condition" (142). This brutal awakening constitutes the ambiguous gift of reason, for rationality is what leads us inevitably to reflection, to an awareness of self, and, thus, ultimately to recognition of our mortality, our historical, temporal being. In this sense, reason is also the motive force of history, driven by a desire for emancipation from its own discovery of death, a desire made possible by our capacity for what Rousseau calls "perfectability." Yet, there is a dreadful irony in this perfectibility. For the further we travel in the pursuit of emancipation from the bonds of our mortality, the further we travel away from the putative calm of our initial state, the further we become creatures of artifice (and, therefore, deception), the further we retreat from a commonly held, if inchoate, world into a world of increasingly disparate individuals that we manufacture for ourselves. In this regard, Rousseau employs a precise and striking metaphor at the beginning of the *Discourse on the Origins and Foundations of Inequality among Men* (1756):

> Like the statue of Glaucus, which time, the seas and the storms had so disfigured that it resembled less a dog than a wild beast, the human soul modified in society by a thousand ever-recurring causes, by the acquisition of a mass of knowledge and errors, by mutations taking place in the constitution of the body, and by the constant impact of the passions, has changed in appearance to the point of becoming almost unrecognizable, and is no longer to be found . . . (124)

Reason, in attempting to free us from the misery occasioned by the knowledge of death it first brings about, only exacerbates that misery. Here is the central contradiction: that the means by which we both recognize and attempt to overcome our misery, our estrangement from the state of nature and its "animal" immortality, assures us, by dint of its limitedness, that we cannot. The final point of history, then, must be the realization of a bind from which there is no escape. If there is indeed any escape, it must be sought through artifice or palliative, a mediating structure that can only help us forget what cannot be otherwise achieved. The darker message is unavoidable: our lot as creatures of history is suffering, an ineradicable dissatisfaction that must settle with a simulacrum of the state of nature, that is, an artifice designed to restrain, not encourage, thought. For Rousseau's complex metaphor of the disfigured statue suggests not only that there is no return to the natural state—the statue is, after all, already a work of artifice—but that there is an artifice that can be more beneficial in averting those tendencies that lead to disfigurement in the first place.[6]

Schopenhauer

Unlike Rousseau, Schopenhauer is not a thinker of history. Rather, he is a thinker of the singular, yet all-encompassing, will that both conceals and reveals itself in the world as the latter appears to us. The will conceals itself in so far as we know objects through representations, that is, as we represent them to ourselves as knowing subjects according to the conditions of time, space, and causality. For Schopenhauer these three conditions determine the identity of any object; they are the basic conditions without which rational cognition of objects would be impossible. The will reveals itself, however, in so far as the mere fact of conditionality suggests that there must be something "there" prior to the conditions, something that is subject to those conditions.

Such a conclusion may seem unduly perplexing at first. Schopenhauer insists that rational cognition is thoroughly representational, that is, conditioned; and yet he also insists on referring to what precedes representation as some thing, even if the identity of that thing must be construed as the obverse of identity, as that which, as the ground of identity, cannot be both the ground of identity and an identity. What is going on here? How does Schopenhauer avoid this looming contradiction? Not surprisingly, Schopenhauer relies on intuition, not reason, to avoid contradiction. He claims that the reliance of reason on conditions entails that reason can only infer that there is something like the will but nothing more. For reason, the will cannot be an object of representation: it is nothing or pure immediacy. But, for intuition, this pure immediacy is vibrant, it is the urge to be itself:

This is a knowledge that the inner nature of his own phenomenon, which manifests itself to him as representation both through his actions and through the permanent substratum of these his body, is his *will*. This will constitutes what is most immediate in his consciousness, but as such it has not wholly entered into the form of the representation, in which object and subject stand over against each other; on the contrary, it makes itself known in an immediate way in which subject and object are not quite clearly distinguished . . . (1/109)

Reason and will are fundamentally at odds. The more reason considers the world, the less it finds itself in it, the more it concludes that the essence of the world lies beyond it, that this essence is simply not rational. Here is the corrosive irony, for reason comes to recognize its own limitation, its own inability to identify itself with the world. Hence, in a way that does recall Rousseau, reason can do little more but serve to turn us away from the essential nature of the world, the will. Reason is once again responsible for estrangement and perplexity. As with Rousseau, art assumes a crucial role, since only art can bring a cessation of the conflict reason first brings to the fore. In so doing, art provides us with a knowledge of the whole as it is that reason simply is unable to achieve because, as conditional, reason is in thrall to the will:

Apprehension of an Idea . . . consists in knowledge turning away entirely from our own will, and thus leaving entirely out of sight the precious pledge entrusted to it, and considering things as though they could never in any way concern the will. For only thus does knowledge become the pure mirror of the objective inner nature of things. A knowledge so conditioned must be the basis of every genuine work of art in its origin. The change in the subject required for this, just because it consists in the elimination of all willing, cannot proceed from the will, and hence cannot be an arbitrary act of will, in other words, cannot rest with us. On the contrary, it springs only from a temporary preponderance of the intellect over the will . . . (2/367)

This "temporary preponderance" is a moment of illumination Schopenhauer associates with genius whose knowledge is "essentially purified of all willing and of references to the will" (2/380). While philosophical thought can lead us to see the peculiar two-sidedness of the world, the conflict between reason and will, representational and nonrepresentational modes of apprehension of the world, it cannot show us what the world is in itself: only art can do that, and music tells us most because it is the least representational of the arts. The profound impact of this thinking on the relation between reason and consciousness in *War and Peace* should be abundantly clear.

***

Both Rousseau and Schopenhauer suggest that reason can achieve only a negative result: it can but articulate its own inadequacy to attain to perfect, synoptic knowledge of the whole, a divinely disinterested contemplation of all that is. To attain this point requires art; philosophy thus depends on the supplement of artistic apprehension if it is to be anything other than a discourse of negation, the nihilism mentioned above. This specific articulation of philosophical inadequacy and dependence within the discourse of philosophy itself is—to adopt Alain Badiou's term—deeply antiphilosophical. Let me explain why this is this so.[7]

Philosophy opposes itself to other attempts to grasp the whole because it seeks to do so through reason alone. A philosophy that does little more than engage in a critique of reason's capacity to know, that circles around the limitations of reason, suggesting that philosophy can tell us only of its own frailty, is still philosophy. Recall here that philosophy is the "love of wisdom," a pursuit of wisdom or synoptic knowledge than can only be a kind of love to the extent the beloved remains unattainable. But a philosophy that engages in a critique of reason in order to indicate that reason cannot attain what can be attained otherwise, say, through religion or art, is a veritable antiphilosophy which employs the conceptual apparatus of philosophy as a way of persuading one to abandon philosophy for something else. In this sense, Schopenhauer is much more of an antiphilosopher than Rousseau, who still gives philosophy an important role in quelling the dissatisfactions it helps to create.

From this perspective, one may argue that Tolstoy is much closer to Schopenhauer than to Rousseau. The difference is, as in all things Tolstoyan, that there is a marked oscillation. But, even when Tolstoy is at his most philosophical, he tends to demand of philosophy that it convert itself from a love of knowledge to knowledge itself: he is never content with simply admiring, for he seeks above all to possess the beloved, and, if possession is impossible he is full of scorn and derision.

While one can glean the basic elements of this position from *A Confession*, where religion ambiguously prevails, one can also glean another view, from Tolstoy's philosophical writings themselves, where art prevails in an equally ambiguous manner. Among these writings, *On Life* and *What is Art?* provide an interesting and illuminating counterpoint.

TOLSTOY'S PHILOSOPHY

On Life is Tolstoy's most purely philosophical work. I use the term "purely" with some hesitation; the work mentions only rather sparingly a central, dogmatic assumption, that the basic teachings of Jesus are rational or entail no conflict between reason and revelation. Be that as it may, the principal assertions advanced by Tolstoy have a far greater affinity with Kant than Jesus: if there is agreement between reason and revelation here, it decisively favors reason.[8]

The basic argument of *On Life* sets out an opposition between two kinds of life: what Tolstoy refers to as the "animal life," that of our "animal personality," and the human life, that of "rational consciousness." The former denotes the life of the individual with all its immediate concerns, a life that seeks the welfare of the individual as against others. The latter denotes the reflective capacity that permits us to think the good, the proper end of human striving. What is this good? It seems to have two basic characteristics: (1) that one place the general welfare over one's own; (2) that, in doing so, one free oneself of the inordinate and ultimately vain concern for one's own body. To think the good is, then, to think the whole by overcoming the distortions of animal interest. For if our animal personality is trapped within the confines of time and space, trapped before the prospect of certain death, and, thus, at once eager and unable to escape that trap, rational consciousness is not subject to time: in the strictest sense, it is outside of time. Hence, to lead a life freed of the torment of death, one must choose to embrace rational consciousness.

The equation of rationality with freedom and the good is a thoroughly Kantian move. For Kant's moral theory makes it quite clear that the prerogatives or inclinations of the body are expressions of enslavement. The body enslaves itself because it is completely dependent on its environment. The body is inherently reactive, various stimuli activate it, and these impose themselves to the extent the body must react to them. Kant calls this kind of enslavement heteronomy, his term for interestedness. In contrast, rationality is active, following its own ends and directing action in accordance with these ends. A rational actor is autonomous, disinterested, unperturbed by the momentary enthusiasms of the body, and the laws by which he or she acts are thus necessarily universal in character: they are capable of being followed by all freely.[9] This is, after all, the governing condition for determining whether an action is rational or not; namely, that the action can be universalized—anyone can perform it—without contradiction, without thereby inflicting harm or inviting destruction. Like Kant, Tolstoy equates the good with rationality and universality.[10] Striving for the good, then, is the privileging of the universal over the particular, the one over the many, rational principle over physical impulse.

This clear privileging dismisses reconciliation between the opposed elements, which boil down to an opposition between the unity of mind and the plurality of the body. Tolstoy seems to reject thereby the primary movement of the great novels and his major Christian writings in favor of advocating a rationalism so radical that it rejects embodiment, which must be overcome in pursuit of the ends set by the mind. Not a few critics took note of the radicality of this suggestion and attacked *On Life* essentially on that level: they noted that Tolstoy's teaching requires the subordination of the (embodied) self to the rational law in such an immoderate manner that Tolstoy's thinking amounts to annihilation of the physical self.[11] There is little to contradict that accusation—is that not the avowed purpose?—namely, to liberate us from our corrupted being, an unstable mixture of physical and mental impulse, deeply at odds with each other, and which do not speak the same language or see the same things.

If suicide is not Tolstoy's central assertion, and it seems dubious that it is, then Tolstoy's argument commits us to continuous striving, the end being impossible to realize.[12] But this flies in the face of Tolstoy's commitment to establishing the kingdom of God on earth. It is, therefore, hard to square the one approach with the other.

Is this the significance of philosophy as opposed to religion? Is philosophy after creating an impossible "city in speech," as Plato wrote, rather than a living city? Is this the main reason why philosophy cannot replace dogma because its largely critical faculties can only project an impossible order? One might answer this question by referring to the peculiarity of *On Life* when considered among Tolstoy's later works. While the fictions and philosophy question their own possibility in ways both subtle and coarse, Tolstoy's Christian teachings avoid such a critical approach.

TOLSTOY'S ANTIPHILOSOPHY

Is Tolstoy, then, an antiphilosopher? One of his most interesting later writings, *What is Art?* stages this question as an instance of philosophy looking at one of its competitors or, in more modern jargon, as philosophy looking at its "other." For is this not what aesthetics as a philosophical inquiry into the nature of art proposes to do? But, if one were to judge from the tradition, one might be led to believe that aesthetics is little more than the appropriation of art by philosophy.[13] The mere fact that philosophy arrogates to itself the position of judgment over the nature of art suggests that philosophy possesses an authority which art does not. And it is hardly a secret that philosophy has rivaled for authority with poetry at least since Plato, whose scathing criticism of poetry was matched by his cunning use of its traditions, conventions, and linguistic innovations in his own dialogues.

From this point of view *What is Art?* presents a fascinating undermining of the philosophical appropriation of art, an often rather grim riposte not only to the pretensions of philosophical discourse on art but to any form of critical or analytic discourse that purports to explain a work of art. Indeed, the main argument of the treatise involves a thoroughgoing refutation of mediating discourses as such, thereby putting even itself in question as belonging to one such discourse, aesthetics.

Before we move to that point, however, let me provide a brief survey of the main argument. This argument involves several stages, of which the first ridicules beauty as the relevant criterion by which the value of a work of art may be determined. Tolstoy engages in such ridicule because he finds the definition of beauty wanting: beauty is that which causes pleasure. And because pleasure is always variable, always subject to caprice and inclination, Tolstoy is unable to grasp how beauty can be, as a prime criterion of artistic merit, anything more than hollow and misleading. Moreover, if beauty is what gives pleasure, then it is hard to make any firm connection between beauty and the good. But Tolstoy pursues an even more radical point here: beauty and the good are not only not identical, they are essentially opposed. Hence, art judged by the criterion of beauty cannot be good, a point already asserted in *The Kreutzer Sonata*, and art that is good cannot be beautiful.

What, then, is good art? Good art has two characteristics, one relating to form, the other to content. From the point of view of form, good art infects. Specifically, good art infects the artist's audience with a feeling the artist experiences and then seeks to express in his art. Formal accomplishment is measured by the capacity of the work to infect its audience: the greater the infection, the greater the formal accomplishment.[14] From the point of view of content, good art infects its audience with a feeling that had hitherto not found expression and which supports and deepens the religious worldview patent or latent within the community to which the artist belongs. Good art thus serves this religious worldview—which can mean merely the basic beliefs that bind a community as such—and therefore plays a central role in maintaining that community. Indeed, the notion of community here is of central significance, for art that is good both in form and content brings about communion (or communication) among people.[15] As Tolstoy notes: "In order to define art precisely, one must first of all cease looking at it as a means of pleasure and consider it as one of the conditions of human life. Considering art in this way, we cannot fail to see that art is a means of communion among people" (30:V//63/37).

This final comment is extremely important. For art to be good it must achieve the aim of creating a communion between artist and audience that allows for a sharing of feeling otherwise impossible to achieve. Art must therefore deploy form and content in such a way that the divisive mediation of form melts away in the experience of art, which is one that cannot properly be described. It follows that critical discourses relating to art have no significance whatsoever. If anything, critical discourses get in the way. They impair the experience of communion, constituting an intrusion of thought into art that diminishes the most important aspect of art, the sharing of feeling. One must be clear on this latter point: Tolstoy maintains that critical discourses can only be harmful, that they undermine the work of art. Moreover, any work of art that requires some critical discourse as an aid to understanding must not be a good work of art.

For a good work of art exhausts itself in the relationship of communion it establishes.

This is a radical position that wishes to return art to a position of authority it has lost. The model, here as elsewhere, is the Bible (if not Homer as well), a writing that overcomes itself, that creates a lasting communion and defies commentary (no matter how many may exist). One reads to be occupied by the work, in less polite language, to yoke oneself to the artist's vision, which happens to be some as yet uncovered aspect of a religious worldview. Tolstoy thereby robs art of autonomy. Put more precisely, art can be beneficially free only in regard to form, the choice of which artistic means best enable the occupation of the audience by the artist's intention. In this sense, art is a means of propagating a religious worldview, only becoming more effective in this task to the extent it protects itself from criticism or has grounds to do so.

This is assuredly not a modern art, not an ironic art, but one that is weighed down by a governing idea that must come from elsewhere. But there is a greater problem concealed in this dependence. How do I know that I have been infected with the vision of the artist? How can I even know I am infected if I cannot articulate in what that infection consists? The movement away from commentary to an ostensibly "pure" writing is much more radical than it seems because the goal of pure communication is one that cannot be verified either in myself or through discussion with others. As soon as I think about the work I turn it into something it is not: I betray, reduce, and lose it. What kind of art can this be but one that is beyond technique, that engages in the desperate task of attempting to communicate in words what can only be lost through them?

There is little new in this thinking. We have encountered it most vividly in the context of Tolstoy's great novels. The hankering for the immediate and unconditioned is the same, but the irony of failure is missing. Unless, of course, we take into account the status of *What is Art?* itself as a treatise. Why does Tolstoy write a philosophical treatise against commentary about art, indeed, against the kind of writing about art in which the treatise engages? If we approach *What is Art?* from this perspective, it appears that philosophy provides the necessary means of speaking to that audience which is the target audience of *What is Art?*, namely, the rich and powerful, the perverse and secular, those who claim that the criterion for aesthetic judgment is beauty. Philosophy, then, is a way of speaking to those who have erred from the truth, that truth being the religious view philosophy is incapable of assimilating completely since it is the discourse of reason, not faith. But how can one gauge that error? How can one even know it?

The irony here is that Tolstoy must affirm the very discursivity he condemns. The need to define art is the strongest evidence that art cannot define itself, that art cannot survive in the prediscursive realm to which Tolstoy longs to return it. The attack against any discourse on art applies equally to any discourse on any object, that is to say, to any form of reflection. Tolstoy's intransigent, antiphilosophical opposition to reflection as the source of doubts, of miscommunication, of error comes to the surface here again, and it reveals its ironies with no less force, if perhaps less explicitly than elsewhere.

THE IMPOSSIBILITY OF PHILOSOPHY

The picture of Tolstoy that emerges from the foregoing discussion is typically inconclusive, revealing conflicting tendencies. On the one hand, Tolstoy was drawn to philosophy because it seemed to offer a comprehensive picture of the world or, at the least, a conclusive framework for grasping our place in the world. On the other hand, Tolstoy's clear apprehension of the limits of reason, which created an ever deeper reserve of suspicion in him regarding philosophy, compelled him to decry its incapacity to answer the simplest questions or, as we saw, to communicate in a meaningful way. In this regard, Wittgenstein's famous rejection of philosophy as being able to provide answers to questions, just not the important ones, bears a striking family resemblance to Tolstoy's.

CHAPTER 6

EPILOGUE

A DEFINITIVE TOLSTOY?

Who, then, is Tolstoy? Is there any incontrovertible answer to this question? Is he a writer of fictions, a charismatic prophet, or a philosopher? Which of these discourses subordinates the others? Which has supreme authority? Which defines Tolstoy?

If one seeks a definitive Tolstoy, one is likely to be disappointed. To impose a definition on Tolstoy or to create a picture of Tolstoy that seeks to impose itself, to foreclose deviating paths of thought, hardly fits Tolstoy's fundamental elusiveness. At best—and this is already a great deal—one can come to appreciate several primary lines of exploration in Tolstoy, which, though they may be complicated by a proliferation of offshoots, of paths quickly taken and abandoned, do permit confrontation with Tolstoy's inexhaustible multiplicity; a confrontation more in tune with Tolstoy's own thinking as expressed, for example, in *War and Peace*, where it is motion, not rest, that retains the power to fascinate.

At the beginning of this book, I suggested that Tolstoy's attitude toward truth may provide a "royal road" into his world. But, in the final account, one may reasonably ask whether this "royal road" leads anywhere or simply is another *Holzweg*, a "path leading nowhere." This is no idle question; it is one that sheds light on the most enigmatic aspects of Tolstoy's inability ever to find rest. For Tolstoy's unceasing quest after truth, as a highest authority or adjudicative center, reflects, it seems to me, a far more profound sense that reconciliation of the one and the many, of the idea and the multitude of experience, of society and individual, is simply impossible. Authority is necessary only where reconciliation cannot be realized other than through some form of fiction or coercion that claims to eliminate the gap between the one and the many. This gap is the perpetual source of disharmony, dissonance, disaffection: the breach in the otherwise beguiling fabric of the world that cannot be closed. The discovery of the infinite serves merely to complicate the matter by ensuring that the one, no matter how capacious, cannot express the many without force or fraud. Hence, while the quest after truth gives a certain order to Tolstoy's multiplicity, the infinite dissolves that order—indeed, it renders it impossible.

Truth is important, the infinite is more so. If one had to identify a governing concept in Tolstoy's works, I would have to maintain that it is the infinite. The impossibility that the infinite inscribes into all striving to grasp the whole is more fundamental to Tolstoy than any other single notion. Without the infinite, the pathos and fecundity of Tolstoy's writings would be incomprehensible, their urgency, variability and rhetorical invention null. Far more than the quest after truth, which is merely the outward reflection of a deeper-lying struggle, the infinite finds itself everywhere in evidence as the fulcrum of Tolstoy's work. In this sense, Tolstoy is one of few great writers to perceive the terrible threat the infinite poses not only to the creations of art but to those of thought and practical action: the infinite is the sign of negation par excellence, it "corrupts and confuses," it frustrates all human endeavor.[1] Wherever one looks in Tolstoy, wherever one seeks an answer in his writings, one finds the infinite.

THREE STRANDS OF INFLUENCE: LITERATURE, POLITICS, AND PHILOSOPHY

The tensions in Tolstoy, however, had far less impact than one might expect, and his legacy in the twentieth century has been marked by an attraction that amounts in many respects almost to a nostalgia for lost authority; a return to literary certainties that many of the most important writers in the twentieth century fought mightily to destroy. Tolstoy's most capable readers tended to be drawn to the absolutes, to be dazzled by the magisterial assurance of Tolstoy's writings rather than by the burgeoning conflicts that lay below the surface. This is perhaps why writers often opposed, and still oppose, Tolstoy to Dostoevsky as antipodes.[2]

In what follows I give a mere sketch of Tolstoy's influence in the twentieth century. Since this influence has been so extraordinarily broad, as befits someone who pursued many different ways of approaching an ever inscrutable world, I concentrate my account on three cases of influence from each of the major discourses discussed in this book: literature, religion, and philosophy.

Literature: The Narrative of War

Although preceded by Stendhal in important respects, Tolstoy almost single-handedly changed the representational language for depicting scenes of war. One of the most significant, and influential, aspects of this change was Tolstoy's focus on the chaotic nature of battle. Rather than describing battle within the traditional ambit of narrative, as having a solid beginning, middle and end, with all the specific parts of the battle woven together in the achievement of the final result, Tolstoy showed just how radically open-ended battles can be, that no one narrative can encompass the complexity of the actions which contribute to the final result. In so doing, Tolstoy adopted an approach that tried to represent, within the narrow narrative limits available to him, that which exceeds narrative limits or, put more bluntly, the ordering principles inherent in them. In other words, Tolstoy creates a new narrative language for scenes of war in so far as he maintains that the chaos of battle brings to the fore the limitations of narrative.

While not all of his successors may have had Tolstoy's evident concern with the limits of narrative in mind, there is nonetheless little question as to the scope of his influence: it has been enormous. Tolstoy's influence on writers of the Soviet period who had ample experience of war, like Isaac Babel, Konstantin Fedin, Vassily Grossman, and Aleksandr Solzhenitsyn, is perhaps only to be expected given the shadow Tolstoy cast over all his successors in his own language. Other cases of influence, like Ernst Jünger and Ernest Hemingway, suggest that Tolstoy's approach to war held a more universal appeal.

The largely formal quality of that appeal becomes clear if one considers the very different political orientations of these writers. For there is little harmony between the views of writers like Babel and Fedin, both working within the Soviet Union, and even less between a man of the right like Jünger and one leaning to the left like Hemingway. All these writers recognized in Tolstoy's description of the chaotic nature of battle a different element to extol, a tribute to the richness and modernity of Tolstoy's approach.

Religion as Politics: Nonviolent Resistance

Tolstoy's call for nonviolent resistance was heeded in a way that few could possibly have predicted. For an obscure Indian lawyer working in South Africa at the end of the nineteenth century began to read Tolstoy. This lawyer was none other than Mohandas Gandhi (1869–1948) who would later become the central figure in India's struggle for independence from British colonial rule. While Gandhi initially found Tolstoy's religious writings of interest for their espousal of vegetarianism and a strict asceticism, he soon came to value Tolstoy's doctrines of nonresistance to evil and peaceful civil disobedience.

These ideas were crucial elements of the Tolstoyan communes that Gandhi established while still in South Africa and which Tolstoy himself praised. Gandhi of course pursued his Tolstoyan thinking when he returned to India in 1915 and initiated a series of popular campaigns where he encouraged Indians not to purchase British products and not to obey the dictates of the colonial administration. In these campaigns the Tolstoyan injunction to nonviolent resistance proved to be a formidable political weapon that forced the British colonial administration into a state of ever increasing confusion and impotence. Moreover, Gandhi's courage and perseverance, his astonishing discipline in face of a foe utterly superior in material resources, set an example for the many thousands of others who joined in the protests, which ultimately led to the devolution of British power in India.

One of Gandhi's admirers was Martin Luther King, Jr and King brought Gandhi's ideas to those civil rights struggles in the United States which are one of the most interesting and important aspects of the early 1960s. While it is uncertain whether King ever read Tolstoy—and, indeed, it is likely that he did not—his adopting of Gandhi's approach to civil disobedience makes him an indirect heir of Tolstoy.

Philosophy: Silence and Death

The two central philosophers of the first half of the twentieth century, Ludwig Wittgenstein and Martin Heidegger, were also influenced in important ways by Tolstoy.

Tolstoy's influence on Wittgenstein seems to have been pervasive. Wittgenstein carried Tolstoy's *Gospel in Brief* with him everywhere during the First World War and credited it with "saving him." But the exact contours of that influence are hard to define. Tolstoy's ethical concerns and praise of simplicity seem to have made a deep impression on the young Wittgenstein, who belonged to a very wealthy Viennese family. Yet it is Tolstoy's concern with the limits of language, with the possibility of achieving knowledge of the most important things through language, that seems to have had a more durable impact. Indeed, as I noted, Wittgenstein's formidable mistrust of philosophy as a way of coming to terms with the world has much in common with Tolstoy: both Tolstoy and Wittgenstein cast doubt on the efficacy of philosophy, on the resources available to the latter to effect change, to address questions that may bring about a new orientation to the world.

In the case of Heidegger, who most likely preferred Dostoevsky,[3] Tolstoy exerted influence mainly through *The Death of Ivan Ilyich*. Heidegger makes direct reference to that story in a famous footnote to his major work *Being and Time* (1927). Heidegger cites Tolstoy in the context of the evasion of death where Heidegger maintains, fully in line with Tolstoy, that "the dying of others is seen often as a social inconvenience, if not a downright tactlessness, from which publicness should be spared." At least one commentator[4] has claimed that Heidegger's discussion of death in *Being and Time* owes a great deal more to Tolstoy than Heidegger indicates, but this is hardly clear. While there may be grounds to argue that Heidegger's position shows a pervasive affinity to that expressed in *The Death of Ivan Ilyich*, notably including the notion that the evasion of death is both problematic *and* necessary, Heidegger's project in *Being and Time* is at once too complex and too intensely original to allow his discussion of death to be so quickly dismissed as a mere gloss on Tolstoy's story.

***

So, to ask again: Who is Tolstoy? Tolstoy is plurality, change and movement. This is arguably his most powerful legacy. For Tolstoy represents a life seeking its limits, ceaselessly inventive, restless and unsure: here is an artist who combines tremendous moral earnestness with cunning and delight in the power fiction grants its creator; here is a questing, religious personality who combines authentic humility with an arrogance that mocks any notion of piety; here is a supreme rationalist whom reason disappoints; here, finally, is a man who sought to become at home in the world and ran away from home to die. The wonder of Tolstoy is that he encompassed all these divergent energies and converted them into an immensely rich body of work that magnificently expresses the sheer precariousness of human life, that homelessness with which we try to become at home despite death's insistent presence.

NOTES

INTRODUCTION: WHAT IS TRUTH?

[1] The apparent irony of seeking truth through a sustained project of creating fictions is never completely absent even when Tolstoy most vociferously rejects fiction; to the contrary, these latter cases may be especially instructive. Vladimir Alexandrov's recent book on *Anna Karenina* offers an excellent discussion of this latter issue. See Alexandrov, *Limits to Interpretation*, 112–33.

[2] As Tolstoy wrote in his diary entry for October 6, 1863: "I am rolling, rolling down the mountain of death and hardly feel in myself the power to stop. I do not want death; I want and love immortality. There is no point in choosing. The choice has long been made" (48:57). This quote is also discussed by Bunin. See Bunin, *The Liberation of Tolstoy*, 123.

[3] An important counterview is that Tolstoy's career is marked by continuous crisis such that it is somewhat unfair to attribute too much importance to one particular, if prolonged, period of crisis, like that which accompanied Tolstoy's Christian conversion in the 1880s, considered the crucial dividing point in his life. See, in particular, Richard Gustafson, *Leo Tolstoy*, 3–52.

[4] I am referring to the once standard "life and works" survey of an author that owed much to nineteenth-century notions of an author's ownership of his texts. According to this view, readers could do little better than ascertain the author's intention in the text in order to discover its legitimate meaning; in other words, a putative intention—a sort of "divine will"—was ascribed to the text, and this intention prescribed in turn the limits of interpretation for that text. This view, holding up the author as "god" of his text, collapsed in the twentieth century along with its theocratic heritage.

[5] The able translator of Nietzsche, Walter Kaufmann, emphasizes the austerity of Tolstoy's views. See Kaufmann, *Religion from Tolstoy to Camus*, 2–3.

[6] Such questions are of a particularly sensitive nature in the Russian context given the rise of Socialist Realism under Stalin in the dark 1930s. Socialist Realism imposed by fiat an ideological structure to which all artistic works worthy of the name were supposed to conform. In his essay, "Catastrophes in the Air," for example, Joseph Brodsky dismisses Tolstoy as a pernicious, destructive influence on modern Russian writing, as the chief

model of those virtues to which Socialist Realism would later aspire. See Brodsky, *Less Than One*, 268–303.

[7] A recent survey of 125 leading writers listed *Anna Karenina* and *War and Peace* as, respectively, the first and third books on a list of the top ten literary works of all time. While one has to be suspicious of such rankings, the placement of Tolstoy so high on the lists of so many eminent writers, among whom one finds Paul Auster, Julian Barnes, Jonathan Franzen, Gail Godwin, Ha Jin, Norman Mailer, and Francine Prose, is indicative of his tremendous authority and pervasive influence.

CHAPTER 1: "WHO AM I?"

[1] All dates given in this chapter follow the Julian calendar, which prevailed in Russia until shortly after the Revolution of 1917. According to this calendar, one has to add 13 days to any given date in order to find the correct correlate in the Gregorian calendar now commonly used throughout the world. Dates given according to the Julian calendar are typically designated as "old style" as opposed to those given in "new style," that is, according to the Gregorian calendar.

[2] A note on Russian names may be in order here. Each Russian name has three components: one's given name, a patronymic, and last name: Sofya Andreevna Tolstaia. The patronymic refers to the father's given name. Thus Sofya Andreevna indicates that her father was called Andrei. Both patronymic and last name differ in form according to gender, with an "a" ending generally marking off the feminine. Russians typically refer to each other in formal situations by using the first name and patronymic.

[3] See Citati, *Tolstoy*, 20.

[4] Optina Pustyn (hermitage) is one of Russia's most famous monasteries. It was a major center of religious activity in the nineteenth century. Aside from Tolstoy, a number of famous writers, including Gogol, Turgenev, and Dostoevsky, visited the monastery. One of its local elders, Father Ambrose (Amvrosy), made a lasting impression on Dostoevsky and is commonly thought to be a model for Zosima in *The Brothers Karamazov*. See Joseph Frank, *Dostoevsky: The Mantle of the Prophet*, 384–6.

[5] The witticism was that Russia had two Tsars, one Romanov, one Tolstoy. The latter's authority derived mainly from his implacable and frequently successful resistance to the oppressive aspects of tsarist autocracy. This resistance emerges distinctively after Tolstoy's conversion in the 1880s.

[6] There are many accounts of these final days. For a general overview A. N. Wilson's and Henri Troyat's biographies are a good place to start. Bunin is magisterial, Bulgakov piquant. Jay Parini has written an interesting fictional account, *The Last Station*. For all, see the respective references in the Works Cited.

[7] He considered dividing his life into seven-year periods and also into three stages. In both cases, religious traditions influenced his choice, emphasizing Tolstoy's desire to fit it into a schema of some kind and to hold his life out as exemplary. See Bunin, *The Liberation of Tolstoy*, 5–7.

⁸ See Lermontov's mocking treatment of Rousseau in *Hero of Our Time*, 63–4; Dostoevsky's *Notes from Underground* features a similar attack. See Dostoevsky, *Notes from Underground*, 39.

⁹ See Eikhenbaum, *The Young Tolstoi*, 7–47.

¹⁰ *Dichtung und Wahrheit* refers to Johann Wolfgang von Goethe's great autobiographical work, which stands as a crucial model for writing one's life as an act of deliberate self-fashioning.

¹¹ The question is: How could I describe myself as that self is in its totality? That which describes must subtract or absent itself from the description as a condition of the description's possibility. In other words, the describing agency differentiates itself from what is being described. If this were not the case, if the describing agency and the description were identical, then it is hard to grasp how any description could be made at all.

¹² As recorded by Nietzsche in a notebook entry (1887–1888). The full citation is: "une croyance presque instinctive chez moi c'est que tout homme puissant ment quand il parle, et à plus forte raison quand il écrit" Nietzsche, 13:19.

¹³ Two months before his death in September 1883, Turgenev used these words in a pleading letter to Tolstoy. By then Turgenev, who was living in Paris and mortally ill with cancer, had become increasingly disturbed by Tolstoy's new, Christian life and his consequent rejection of literature. See Turgenev, *Polnoe sobranie sochinenie* XIII:2:180.

¹⁴ On the issue of realism, the literary depiction of reality, see Jakobson, *Language in Literature*, 19–27. As to Tolstoy, one has to be careful not to go too far, to an extreme that would reject the authority of experience merely because it is sifted through various filters. There is a difference between a tale written by someone who experienced the subject matter of the tale and one written by someone who did not; there is a difference between standing in front of a loaded gun and merely imagining oneself to be doing so. To suggest otherwise devalues all testimonial accounts, for example, of camp life either in the Nazi or Stalinist world. But this crucial difference works itself out in literature as a largely ethical restriction on the profligacy of the literary imagination. For literature can be disturbing from this perspective precisely because imagination can steal authority from experience, can fashion it so as to make the imagined account the more persuasive, powerful one. Tolstoy's works combine a keen awareness of this problem—Tolstoy's vaunted capacity to "make it strange," to which I shall later refer, is just such an effort to wrest authority from experience—together with strong misgivings about the power of literature to create such seductive lies, that is, to usurp the authority of experience by creating it anew.

¹⁵ This is an ironic twist, as the connection of disease with creative activity is a staple of the romantic literature for which Tolstoy had little, if any, sympathy.

¹⁶ Robert Louis Jackson gives a particularly interesting account of this crucial incident in Tolstoy's life in terms of the execution scene that is a centerpiece of Pierre's journey in *War and Peace*. See Jackson, *Dialogues with Dostoevsky*, 55–74.

[17] This comes from a letter to Nikolai Strakhov dated March 25, 1873, which Tolstoy did not send (62:16).

[18] *Anna Karenina*, like *War and Peace*, and many other significant Russian novels of the nineteenth century, was first published serially (in Mikhail Katkov's *Russian Herald*) from 1875 to 1877 and completed in book form only in 1878. William Todd's article, "Anna on the Installment Plan: Teaching *Anna Karenina* through the History of its Serial Publication" is worth consulting for more detail. See Knapp and Mandelker, *Approaches to Teaching*, 53–9.

[19] Sir Isaiah Berlin will follow this line of thinking in his famous essay on *War and Peace* in so far as the Faustian Tolstoy resembles one who would like to impose the hegemony of theory over all things. The other, rather more Buddhist, Tolstoy would seek to let things be, to let them appear as they are, somehow freed of the claims that our interestedness makes on them.

[20] F. W. J. Schelling, *Philosophical Investigations*, 63.

[21] To forestall complaints that this is a too "postmodern" view (however one seeks to define that vexed term), or one egregiously tainted by Derridean routes of thought, I point to the following aphorism from Wittgenstein, who, to my knowledge, has not been grouped together with the postmoderns (and who of course admired Tolstoy a very great deal): "Yet if one says: 'How am I supposed to know what he means, I can see only his signs,' then I say: 'How is he supposed to know what he means, for he also has only his signs.'" See Ludwig Wittgenstein, *The Big Typescript*, 4.

[22] This way of looking at the problem of authority in authorship has become (arguably too) commonplace in modern interpretive practice. While Martin Heidegger is one of the key sources of this thinking, as are structuralism and the New Criticism, the famous essays by Michel Foucault ("What is an Author?") and Roland Barthes ("The Death of the Author") carried the day to such an extent that one can speak of authorial authority now only with great caution.

[23] This is an important theme in much twentieth-century thinking about language and language in literature from the Russian Formalists to Heidegger and Jacques Derrida.

CHAPTER 2: A NOVELIST?

[1] This phrase is taken from a remarkable essay Tolstoy published in 1868, called "A Few Words Apropos of the Book *War and Peace*," in which he distinguishes *War and Peace* as a *sui generis* work connected neither to the novel nor to the conventions of historical writing. (This essay is included in the Pevear and Volokhonsky translation at pp. 1217–24.) As to *The Cossacks*, generic definition is complicated by the secondary title, "A Tale of the Caucasus in 1852," which imposes a generic classification that seems to be the object of parody within the text itself. See C. J. G. Turner's article, "Tolstoy's *The Cossacks*: The Question of Genre."

[2] Gary Saul Morson's notion of "negative narration" is an incisive way of describing this technique. See Morson, *Hidden in Plain View*, 130–89.

[3] One is reminded here of Walter Benjamin's comment that ". . . all great works of literature establish a genre or dissolve one . . . they are, in other words, special cases." See Benjamin, *Selected Writings*, 237.

[4] See Harold Bloom, *The Western Canon*, 1.

[5] By "divine intuition" I mean the *visio Dei* [vision of God] or *intuitus originarius* [originating vision] of largely Medieval origin, which considered the primary difference between divine and human cognitive abilities as qualitative. For God's vision is immediate, timeless, infinite, *and* complete. See Martin Heidegger, *Metaphysical Foundations*, 45.

[6] Recall Arthur Schopenhauer's famous opening to his masterwork, *The World as Will and Representation*, where he writes: " 'The world is my representation': this is a truth valid with reference to every living and knowing being, although man alone can bring it into reflective, abstract consciousness. If he really does so, philosophical discernment has dawned on him. It then becomes clear and certain to him that he does not know a sun and an earth, but only an eye that sees a sun, a hand that feels an earth . . ." (1:3).

[7] See both Mikhail Bakhtin and Milan Kundera in the Works Cited. The latter writes: "In the absence of the Supreme Judge, the world suddenly appeared in its fearsome ambiguity; the single divine Truth decomposed into myriad relative truths parceled out by men. Thus was born the world of the Modern Era, and with it the novel, the image and model of that world" (6). Bakhtin associates "unfinalizability" with the novel, negatively defined as an inability ever to achieve the kind of view that is closed and final, beyond perspective or situation within a specific context. It is interesting to note that Bakhtin did not hold Tolstoy in high regard as a novelist precisely because he chose to recognize only the impetus toward closure in Tolstoy's novels. See Bakhtin, *Problems of Dostoevsky's Poetics*, 69–72.

[8] This overly quoted phrase is from Henry James.

[9] See Bloom, *The Western Canon*, 335–6.

[10] Jorge Luis Borges attributes this idea to Novalis. See Borges, *Selected Non-Fictions*, 191.

[11] See Donna Orwin, *Tolstoy's Art and Thought 1847–1880*, 85–98, for a nuanced view of this hesitancy. In general, Orwin's interpretation provides a useful counterweight to the one presented here.

[12] See Richard Gustafson, *Leo Tolstoy*, 54–62.

[13] See Orwin, *Tolstoy's Art and Thought 1847–1880*, 39. The *Symposium* is the more commonly discussed Platonic dialogue in Tolstoy scholarship. Critics have noted how the division of love in that dialogue between purely physical *eros* and an *eros* that strives for a vision of the forms, an idealized erotic drive, seems to fit Tolstoy very well.

[14] See Susan Layton's treatment of these themes in her excellent book and, in particular, her discussion of *The Cossacks* on pp. 240–51.

[15] See note 7 above. Here is the crucial question: Is Tolstoy merely attacking one kind of representation, that of the romantics, or any form of representation?

[16] See John Bayley, *Tolstoy and the Novel*, 266–7; Edward Wasiolek, *Tolstoy's Major Fiction*, 52–4.

[17] Sophia as a figure of wisdom partakes of a complicated tradition in Eastern Orthodox thought. Beatrice guides Dante through the whole of the *Divine Comedy*: she is faith. The "Eternal-feminine" (*das Ewig-Weibliche*) is mentioned at the end of Goethe's *Faust* as a figure inviting a sort of erotic communion with the ideal that recalls Plato.

[18] See Jean-Jacques Rousseau, *The Discourses*, 99–100.

[19] Goethe, *Faust I & II*, 10.

[20] Memorably stated by Henry Wooten in *The Picture of Dorian Gray*.

[21] See Wasiolek, *Tolstoy's Major Fiction*, 52–64, for a careful discussion of this issue.

[22] See Wasiolek, *Tolstoy's Major Fiction*, 54–6; Orwin, *Tolstoy's Art and Thought 1847–1880*, 86–93; Gustafson, *Leo Tolstoy*, 57–8.

[23] Sigmund Freud, *Civilization and Its Discontents*, 11.

[24] There are many notable examinations of this tendency. Hans Blumenberg's magnificent study, *The Legitimacy of the Modern Age*, is an excellent place to start. In this connection, one may also refer to the classic text of Theodor Adorno and Max Horkheimer, *The Dialectic of Enlightenment*, as well as the works of Leo Strauss listed in the Works Cited.

[25] This point is due to George Steiner.

[26] I am reminded of Gorky's observations about Tolstoy himself regarding both his cunning and his silence. While Kutuzov is surely not a double for Tolstoy—this being a brand of speculation whose precarious nature has already been discussed—the portrait of Tolstoy given by Gorky has many traits in common with the Kutuzov of *War and Peace*. Moreover, the distinction between Olympian and Russian god that informs Gorky's comments also seems applicable to the different kinds of approaches to the world that distinguish Napoleon from Kutuzov.

[27] Heidegger remarks, in his famous lectures published as *What Is Called Thinking*: "Interest, *interesse*, means to be among and in the midst of things, or to be at the center of a thing and to stay with it." See Heidegger, *What Is Called Thinking*, 5.

[28] The concept of "wu wei" in Chinese thought has striking affinity with this Tolstoyan notion of passivity. See Michael Denner's article, "Tolstoyan Nonaction: The Advantage of Doing Nothing," listed in the Works Cited.

[29] Witold Gombrowicz remarks, in regard to Schopenhauer's notion of genius: "*The genius is disinterested. He has fun with the world.*" See Gombrowicz, *A Guide to Philosophy*, 34.

[30] See Jackson, "Pierre and Dolochov at the Barrier: The Lesson of the Duel."

[31] Pierre's embrace of radical politics at the end of the First Epilogue seems to indicate that he will become a "Decembrist," a group, made up primarily of aristocrats with liberal ideas, that initiated a clumsy attempt to overthrow Nicholas I upon his accession to the throne in December 1825 (hence, their name). While few of these conspirators were killed, many were sent to Siberia for long exiles. The repetition here of Pierre's most outrageously willful act, his attempt to kill Napoleon, should be obvious, and thus a sign of his rejection of the Kutuzovian orientation, which he received in the more radical variant presented by Platon Karataev.

[32] See A. V. Knowles, *Tolstoy: The Critical Heritage*, 89–198.

[33] Christian's discussion of Tolstoyan repetition is a useful introduction. See Christian, *Tolstoy's "War and Peace"*, 130–7; Natasha Sankovitch supplies greater detail and breadth.

[34] Here the difference is between an essentially Aristotelian notion of narrative and a modern one that takes its cues from mathematical models. See Jeff Love, *The Overcoming of History*, 80–3.

[35] See Love, *The Overcoming of History*, 58–95.

[36] See Borges, *Selected Non-Fictions*, 339.

[37] Vilém Flusser, summarizing a vast tradition, writes: "Human communication is an artistic technique whose intention it is to make us forget the brutal meaningless of a life condemned to death . . . human communication spins a veil around us in the form of a codified world." See Flusser, *Writings*, 4.

[38] The epigraph has been the object of intense scholarly inquiry. See, for example, Kate Holland's article: "The Opening to *Anna Karenina*"; also Alexandrov, *Limits to Interpretation*, 67–70.

[39] See Morson, *Hidden in Plain View*, 9–20.

[40] Nabokov was the first to make this point, which Alexandrov elaborates nicely. See Alexandrov, *Limits to Interpretation*, 71–3.

[41] There is nothing new in this approach, it is practically commonplace both inside and outside of Tolstoy scholarship. One "outsider," Walter Kaufmann, has written eloquently about the fundamental role that deception and, in particular, self-deception plays in the novel (in *Existentialism, Religion and Death*, 15–27).

[42] There are two master texts here, *On the Advantage and Disadvantage of History for Life*, and the much more powerful *On the Genealogy of Morality*. In the latter work, one of the great philosophical works of the German tradition and perhaps Nietzsche's most important work, the second treatise begins with a striking reflection on the role of forgetfulness. See Nietzsche, *On the Genealogy of Morality*, 35–6.

[43] One can argue that Vronsky somehow becomes aware at the end of the novel. But his misery is still ambiguous: Is his not the misery of a wounded animal?

[44] Borges, *Selected Non-Fictions*, 259.

[45] Morson makes an interesting distinction here, suggesting that it is Anna's attribution of predictive authority to these events that is problematic not the events themselves. Anna confers a fatal meaning on events that they cannot bear. See Morson, "Anna Karenina's Omens" in Allen and Morson, *Freedom and Responsibility*, 134–52.

[46] See Nietzsche, *The Birth of Tragedy*, 33–41.

[47] See Alexandrov, *Limits to Interpretation*, 107–11.

[48] The association of wisdom with Plato is unmistakable, especially given the reference to that other wise Plato, Platon Karataev, from *War and Peace*. But the distinction is also intriguing. Although Plato is a most elusive philosopher, never speaking in his own voice in his dialogues, it is relatively safe to assert that there is a peculiar, telling irony here, since that Plato would never have written anything had he accepted Platon Fokanych's perspective. And, indeed, the same goes for Tolstoy.

⁴⁹ One is reminded of Erich Heller's comment on tradition, that "[t]radition is the wise agreement not to ask certain questions, to narrow the domain of the questionable, and grant the mind a firm foundation of answers which can be taken for granted." See, Heller, 14, and the discussion of *A Confession* below.

⁵⁰ I paraphrase here a famous letter, dated January 27, 1878, which Tolstoy wrote to S. A. Rachinsky in response to the latter's complaint about the "deficient construction of the novel" (62:377).

⁵¹ Letter to Nikolai Strakhov dated April 23 and 26, 1876 (62:268).

⁵² To my knowledge, David Herman is the first to have examined the importance of silence in *Hadji Murat*, and I recommend his article, "Khadzhi-Murat's Silence," which tends in a direction rather different from the one I pursue here. As to enthusiasm about the novel, I have only to quote Harold Bloom who calls it "the best story in the world." See Bloom, *The Western Canon*, 336.

⁵³ Bloom, *The Western Canon*, 341.

⁵⁴ Of course, one may argue that Hadji Murat is also a synthesis of these three heroes, evincing at once the anger of Achilles, the protective force of Hector, and the cunning of Odysseus. But this comparison can only go so far. If Hadji Murat does share traits with all three, he belongs to none in his entirety.

⁵⁵ I am reminded of the "innocence of becoming" that Nietzsche describes in connection with the noble type of human being, one freed of the restraints imposed by gloomy self-consciousness. See Nietzsche, *Will to Power*, 400–3, 416.

⁵⁶ There may be some objection to this point, since Hadji Murat thinks carefully before choosing to die. But there is no direct evidence in the text of a reflective, explicitly moral choice, like those which Tolstoy's afflicted heroes attempt to make and which is the essence of a free choice. Rather, the fact that the narrative is generally silent about Hadji Murat's consciousness recommends a different view or one that is skeptical in regard to issues of moral agency.

⁵⁷ See Shklovsky, *Theory of Prose*, 6–9.

CHAPTER 3: A FABULIST?

¹ See Kundera, *Art of the Novel*, 3–20.

² I use the term "short works" here with some hesitation. All of these stories, excluding "How Much Land Does a Man Need?," which is very short, belong uneasily somewhere between what we might call a "long" short story, a novella or a short novel. The Russian term that applies best to these stories is *povest'*, often rendered as "a long tale," but this term is sufficiently broad to cover both the stories and *The Cossacks*, a somewhat longer work. See Kåre Johan Mjør, *Desire, Death and Imitation*, 9–10.

³ Critical opinion has been divided on this beginning, on its role in the emplotment of the story, since it seems to some so little congruous with what follows. See Gary Jahn's introductory comments in his edited volume on the story. Jahn (ed.), *Tolstoy's Death of Ivan Il'ich: A Critical Compan-*

ion, 16–21. The secondary literature on *The Death of Ivan Ilyich* is enormous, and I recommend Jahn's edited volume as a helpful starting point. Jahn's book-length study of the story is worth consulting as are Wasiolek and Gustafson. Also see Inessa Medzhibovskaya's article listed in the Works Cited.

4 Russian formalist thinking provides useful concepts with which to explore the intriguing narrative structure of this work. The distinction between "fabula" and "syuzhet," which, roughly speaking, recognizes that a narrative may articulate temporal units, the "fabula," in a way other than that which typically defines the temporal organization of a specific subject matter, the "syuzhet," applies nicely to the inversion with which *The Death of Ivan Ilyich* begins.

5 Here I direct the reader again to the quote from Flusser above in note 37 to Chapter 2.

6 One wonders how Ivan Ilyich compares to Hadji Murat, who, in quite a different way, is arguably equally inert, equally free of reflection. To be sure, this connection is an uncommon one, but the underlying lack of reflexivity links them.

7 For an interesting perspective on this issue, see Wasiolek, *Tolstoy's Major Fiction*, 169–70.

8 See, for example, Jahn (ed.), *Tolstoy's Death of Ivan Il'ich: A Critical Companion*, 25.

9 This paradox is of importance to *War and Peace*, where the narrator explicitly mentions it in connection with grasping history as continuous motion in the opening chapter of Part 3 of Book III. Regarding desire, I recommend Slavoj Žižek's discussion of Zeno in his *Looking Awry*.

10 See Alexandrov, *Limits to Interpretation*, 141–4.

11 As in *Anna Karenina*; also a very Dostoevskian view, expressed both in *Crime and Punishment* and the short work, "Bobok."

12 See Wittgenstein, *Philosophical Investigations*, 92e–94e (sections 257–265). These sections form a key part of Wittgenstein's celebrated argument against "private language." The problem is a crucial one: How do I express how I feel in a language that cannot be mine?

13 The "Afterword" Tolstoy appended to the story, in which he praises chastity, tends to encourage attitudes of suspicion about the weight of ideology in it.

14 See Kant, *Groundwork*, 95, and Sade's pamphlet, "Frenchmen, Some More Effort If You Wish To Become Republicans" in *Philosophy in the Boudoir*, 104–49.

15 See Gorky, *Reminiscences*, 13.

16 There are strong echoes of Schopenhauerian resignation in this aspect of the story and also, more surprisingly, of Sade's misanthropy. In regard to the former, see the useful overview of Schopenhauer's influence on Tolstoy in Orwin, *Tolstoy's Art and Thought 1847–1880*, 150–164; in regard to the latter, see Lester Crocker's discussion in his *Nature and Culture* at pp. 398–429.

17 See, especially, Schopenhauer, *The World as Will*, 2:447–57.

18 See Strauss, *Plato's Symposium*, 17–24.

[19] See discussion of the *Phaedrus* in the study of *The Cossacks* in Chapter 2.

[20] Tacitus, *Annals*, 386. The phrase comes from Book XV, section 53. The original reads: "cupido dominandi cunctis affectibus flagrantior est." I have modified the translation.

[21] Kant's terms here are phenomena and noumena, the former something that appears in experience, the latter the ground or origin of that appearance. Very roughly speaking, Kant assumes there must be a ground or origin of an appearance that is not equivalent to that appearance because the latter is what it is only through a complex mediating process, one whereby raw "inputs" are transformed into knowable data (representations, which are appearances) by the conceptual apparatus of the understanding. If only appearances are knowable, then the ground of those appearances must remain unknowable: the ground is thus merely an inference, a creature purely of thought, not experience.

[22] Alexandre Kojève, *Reading of Hegel*, 4.

[23] Note that Dickens' story has been connected to the *Death of Ivan Ilyich* where the conversion seems far less convincing than it is in *Master and Man*. See Philip Rogers' article, "Scrooge on the Neva: Dickens and Tolstoy's *Death of Ivan Il'ich*" in Jahn (ed.), *Tolstoy's Death of Ivan Il'ich: A Critical Companion*, 134–67.

CHAPTER 4: A PROPHET?

[1] See Schelling, *Philosophical Investigations*, xi–xxvi; also see Neiman, *Evil in Modern Thought*, 14–109.

[2] Prominent among whom are Weisbein and Walicki. Orwin also stresses Tolstoy's rationalism, although she does not directly deal with the period in question in her book.

[3] This dream is remarkable in itself. It is a cosmic dream in the most literal sense (the Greek *kosmos*, world, is a finite one), for it weaves together a fictional shelter against the infinite whose disruptive quality Tolstoy identifies so effectively in the main part of *A Confession*.

[4] See Janik and Toulmin, *Wittgenstein's Vienna*, 200–1.

CHAPTER 5: A PHILOSOPHER?

[1] See Heidegger, *The Question Concerning Technology* in *Basic Writings*, 341.

[2] "Se moquer de la philosophie, c'est vraiment philosopher." See Pascal, *Oeuvres complètes*, 744.

[3] Žižek, *Organs without Bodies*, 29.

[4] For a very good discussion of both, see Orwin, *Tolstoy's Art and Thought 1847–1880*, 36–49, 150–64. Orwin emphasizes that Plato also had a significant impact on Tolstoy, who read a French translation of the dialogues while stationed in the Caucasus in the early 1850s.

[5] Heidegger notes: "Philosophy, as a human thing, intrinsically fails; and God needs no philosophy." See Heidegger, *Metaphysical Foundations*, 76.

6 Velkley, *Being After Rousseau*, 36–9.

7 Badiou adopts this term from Jacques Lacan to describe those (apparently post-Hegelian) "sophists" who, in the name of philosophy, deny its authority as an independent truth discourse. Among these sophists are Nietzsche, Wittgenstein and Heidegger. See Badiou, 113–38. See also Orwin, "Tolstoy's Antiphilosophical Philosophy in *Anna Karenina*" in Knapp and Mandelker, *Approaches to Teaching*, 95–103.

8 In this respect, *On Life* is an interesting response to *A Confession*. It is also closely linked to *The Death of Ivan Ilyich*, which Tolstoy was writing at the same time. See, in general, Scanlon and Medzhibovskaya in the Works Cited. Also see, in the latter connection, Jahn, *The Death of Ivan Ilich: An Interpretation*, 93–102.

9 Regarding both heteronomy and autonomy, see Kant, *Groundwork*, 108–9, especially Paton's commentary on pp. 37–40.

10 I should note that Tolstoy also radicalizes the Kantian thesis in a way similar to Schelling, one of Kant's most important successors, by maintaining that the striving for the good is at once also a striving toward one's true self, which is immaterial and eternal. See Schelling, *Philosophical Investigations*, 51–3 and Scanlon, "Tolstoy among the Philosophers," 56.

11 See Scanlon, "Tolstoy among the Philosophers," 58–67.

12 Scanlon notes an interesting difference between Kant and Tolstoy in this respect. See Scanlon, "Tolstoy among the Philosophers," 58.

13 See Jean-Marie Schaeffer, *Art of the Modern Age*, 3–13.

14 Caryl Emerson notes three characteristics with which to judge the comparative here: definiteness, clarity, and sincerity. See Emerson's chapter, entitled "Tolstoy's Aesthetics," in *The Cambridge Companion to Tolstoy* at p. 239.

15 Ibid. p. 239. The Russian, *obshchenie*, can mean both communion and communication.

CHAPTER 6: EPILOGUE

1 See Borges' essay "Avatars of the Tortoise" in *Other Inquisitions*, 109–15.

2 Steiner makes the point nicely: "The choice between Tolstoy and Dostoevsky foreshadows what existentialists would call *un engagement*; it commits the imagination to one or the other of two radically opposed interpretations of man's fate, of the historical future, and of the mystery of God" (11).

3 According to Karl Löwith, Heidegger had two portraits on his desk (in the early 1920s): one of Pascal, the other of Dostoevsky. See Löwith, *My Life in Germany*, 30. Heidegger begins the lengthy essay on nihilism in his Nietzsche volumes with an excerpt from Dostoevsky's famous speech about Pushkin.

4 See Kaufmann, *Existentialism, Religion and Death*, 22.

WORKS CITED

TOLSTOY'S WORKS

(a) In Russian

Polnoe sobranie sochinenii. 90 vols. Moscow: Gosudarstvennoe izdatel'stvo, 1928–1958.

(b) In English

Anna Karenina. Trans. Richard Pevear and Larissa Volokhonsky. New York: Penguin, 2000.
A Confession. Trans. David Patterson. New York: W. W. Norton & Company, 1996.
The Cossacks. Trans. David Constantine. New York: Random House, 2004.
The Death of Ivan Ilyich. Trans. Ann Pasternak Slater. New York: Random House, 2003.
"The Gospel in Brief" in *A Confession, The Gospel in Brief and What I Believe*. Trans. Aylmer Maude. London: Oxford University Press, 1940.
Hadji-Murat. Trans. Hugh Alpin. London: Hesperus Press, 2003.
"How Much Land Does a Man Need?" in *How Much Land Does a Man Need? And Other Stories*. Trans. Ronald Wilks. London: Penguin, 1993.
The Kingdom of God Is within You. Trans. Constance Garnett. Lincoln: University of Nebraska Press, 1984.
"The Kreutzer Sonata" in *Tolstoy's Short Fiction*. Ed. with revised trans. by Michael R. Katz. New York: W. W. Norton & Company, 1991.
Master and Man. Trans. Ann Pasternak Slater. New York: Random House, 2003.
On Life. Trans. Aylmer Maude. London: Oxford University Press, 1934.
War and Peace. Trans. Richard Pevear and Larissa Volokhonsky. New York: Knopf, 2007.
"What I Believe" in *A Confession, The Gospel in Brief and What I Believe*. Trans. Aylmer Maude. London: Oxford University Press, 1940.
What Is Art? Trans. Richard Pevear and Larissa Volokhonsky. London: Penguin, 1995.

SECONDARY WORKS

Adorno, T. and Horkeimer, M. *The Dialectic of Enlightenment.* Trans. E. Jephcott. Stanford: Stanford University Press, 2002.

Alexandrov, Vladimir E. *Limits to Interpretation: The Meanings of "Anna Karenina."* Madison: The University of Wisconsin Press, 2004.

Allen, Elizabeth Cheresh and Morson, Gary Saul, eds. *Freedom and Responsibility in Russian Literature: Essays in Honor of Robert L. Jackson.* Evanston: Northwestern University Press, 1995.

Badiou, Alain. *Manifesto for Philosophy.* Trans. Norman Madarasz. Albany: State University of New York Press, 1999.

Bakhtin, M. M. *Problems of Dostoevsky's Poetics.* Ed. and Trans. Caryl Emerson. Minneapolis: The University of Minnesota Press, 1984.

Bayley, John. *Tolstoy and the Novel.* Chicago: The University of Chicago Press, 1966.

Benjamin, Walter. *Selected Writings: Volume 2, Part 1, 1927–1930.* Ed. Michael W. Jennings, Howard Eiland, and Gary Smith. Trans. Rodney Livingstone and others. Cambridge, Mass.: Harvard University Press, 1999.

Berlin, Isaiah. *The Hedgehog and the Fox.* Harmondsworth: Penguin, 1956.

Bloom, Harold. *The Western Canon: The Books and School of the Ages.* New York: Harcourt, Brace & Company, 1994.

Blumenberg, Hans. *The Legitimacy of the Modern Age.* Trans. Robert W. Wallace. Cambridge, Mass.: MIT Press, 1983.

Borges, Jorge Luis. *Other Inquisitions 1937–1952.* Trans. Ruth L. C. Simms. Austin: University of Texas Press, 1964.

—— *Selected Non-Fictions.* Trans. Esther Allen, Suzanne Jill Levine, and Eliot Weinberger. New York: Penguin, 1999.

Brodsky, Joseph. *Less Than One: Selected Essays.* New York: Farrar, Straus, Giroux, 1986.

Bulgakov, Valentin. *The Last Year of Leo Tolstoy.* Trans. Ann Dunnigan. New York: The Dial Press, 1971.

Bunin, Ivan. *The Liberation of Tolstoy: A Tale of Two Writers.* Ed. and Trans. Thomas Marullo and Vladimir Khmelkov. Evanston: Northwestern University Press, 2001.

Christian, R. F. (ed. and trans.). *Tolstoy's "War and Peace."* Oxford: Oxford University Press, 1962.

—— *Tolstoy's Diaries.* 2 vols. London: Athlone Press, 1985.

Citati, Pietro. *Tolstoy.* Trans. Raymond Rosenthal. New York: Schocken Books, 1986.

Crocker, Lester B. *Nature and Culture: Ethical Thought in the French Enlightenment.* Baltimore: The Johns Hopkins Press, 1963.

Denner, Michael. "Tolstoyan Nonaction: The Advantage of Doing Nothing." *Tolstoy Studies Journal.* 13 (2001) 8–22.

Dostoevsky, Fyodor. *Notes from Underground.* Trans. Richard Pevear and Larissa Volokhonsky. New York: Vintage, 1994.

Eikhenbaum, Boris. *The Young Tolstoi.* Trans. Gary Kern. Ann Arbor: Ardis, 1972.

Flusser, Vilém. *Writings*. Ed. Andreas Ströhl. Trans. Erik Eisel. Minneapolis: University of Minnesota Press, 2002.

Frank, Joseph. *Dostoevsky: The Mantle of the Prophet, 1871–1881*. Princeton: Princeton University Press, 2002.

Freud, Sigmund. *Civilization and Its Discontents*. Trans. James Strachey. New York: W. W. Norton & Company, 1961.

Goethe, Johann Wolfgang von. *Faust I & II*. Trans. Stuart Atkins. Princeton: Princeton University Press, 1994.

Gombrowicz, Witold. *A Guide to Philosophy in Six Hours and Fifteen Minutes*. Trans. Benjamin Ivry. New Haven: Yale University Press, 2004.

Gorky, Maksim. *Reminiscences of Tolstoy, Chekhov and Andreyev*. Trans. S. S. Koteliansky and Leonard Woolf. New York: The Viking Press, 1959.

Gustafson, Richard. *Leo Tolstoy: Resident and Stranger*. Princeton: Princeton University Press, 1986.

Heidegger, Martin. *What Is Called Thinking?* Trans. J. Glenn Gray. New York: Harper & Row, 1968.

—— *The Metaphysical Foundations of Logic*. Trans. Michael Heim. Bloomington: Indiana University Press, 1984.

—— *Basic Writings*. Ed. David Farrell Krell. 2nd edn. New York: Harper Collins, 1997.

——. *Introduction to Metaphysics*. Trans. Gregory Fried and Richard Polt. New Haven: Yale University Press, 2000.

Heller, Erich. *The Ironic German: A Study of Thomas Mann*. Boston: Little, Brown and Company, 1958.

Herman, David. "Khadzhi-Murat's Silence." *Slavic Review*. 64 (1) (Spring 2005) 1–23.

Jackson, Robert Louis. "Pierre and Dolochov at the Barrier: The Lesson of the Duel." *Scando-Slavica*. 39 (1993) 52–61.

—— *Dialogues with Dostoevsky*. Stanford: Stanford University Press, 1994.

Jahn, Gary (ed.). *The Death of Ivan Ilych: An Interpretation*. New York: Twayne Publishers, 1993.

—— *Tolstoy's Death of Ivan Il'ich: A Critical Companion*. Evanston: Northwestern University Press, 1999.

Jakobson, Roman. *Language in Literature*. Cambridge, Mass.: Harvard Univeristy Press, 1987.

Janik, Allan and Toulmin, Stephen. *Wittgenstein's Vienna*. Chicago: Ivan R. Dee, 1996.

Kant, Immanuel. *Groundwork of the Metaphysic of Morals*. Trans. H. J. Paton. New York: Harper & Row, 1964.

Kaufmann, Walter (ed.). *Existentialism, Religion and Death: Thirteen Essays*. Signet: New York, 1976.

—— *Religion from Tolstoy to Camus*. New Brunswick: Transaction Publishers, 1994.

Knapp, Liza and Mandelker, Amy. *Approaches to Teaching Tolstoy's Anna Karenina*. New York: The Modern Language Association of America, 2003.

Knowles, A.V. (ed.). *Tolstoy: The Critical Heritage*. London: Routledge and Keegan Paul, 1978.

Kojève, Alexandre. *Introduction to the Reading of Hegel*. Trans. James H. Nichols, Jr. Ithaca: Cornell University Press, 1969.

Kundera, Milan. *Art of the Novel*. Trans. Linda Asher. 2nd edn. New York: Harper Perennial, 2000.

Layton, Susan. *Russian Literature and Empire*. Cambridge: Cambridge University Press, 1994.

Lermontov, M. Yu. *Hero of Our Time*. Trans. Vladimir Nabokov in collaboration with Dmitri Nabokov. Ann Arbor: Ardis, 1988.

Love, Jeff. *The Overcoming of History in War and Peace*. New York, Amsterdam: Rodopi, 2004.

Löwith, Karl. *My Life in Germany Before and After 1933*. Trans. Elizabeth King. Urbana: University of Illinois Press, 1994.

Mandelker, Amy. *Framing Anna Karenina: The Woman Question and the Victorian Novel*. Columbus: Ohio State University Press, 1993.

Marks, Steven G. *How Russia Shaped the Modern World: From Art to Anti-Semitism, Ballet to Bolshevism*. Princeton: Princeton University Press, 2003.

McLean, Hugh (ed.). *In the Shade of the Giant: Essays on Tolstoy*. Berkeley: University of California Press, 1989.

Medzhibovskaya, Inessa. "Teleological Striving and Redemption in *The Death of Ivan Il'ich*." *Tolstoy Studies Journal*. 12 (2000) 35–49.

Mjør, Kåre Johan. *Desire, Death and Imitation*. Slavica Bergensia 4. Bergen: Department of Russian Studies, 2002.

Morson, Gary Saul. *Hidden in Plain View: Narrative and Creative Potentials in "War and Peace."* Stanford: Stanford UP, 1987.

—— *"Anna Karenina" in Our Time*. New Haven: Yale University Press, 2007.

Nabokov, V. V. *Lectures on Russian Literature*. San Diego: Harcourt Brace Jovanovich, 1981.

Neiman, Susan. *Evil in Modern Thought: An Alternative History of Philosophy*. Princeton: Princeton University Press, 2002.

Nietzsche, Friedrich W. *The Birth of Tragedy and The Case of Wagner*. Trans. Walter Kaufmann. New York: Vintage, 1967.

—— *The Will to Power*. Trans. R. J. Hollingdale and Walter Kaufmann. New York: Vintage, 1967.

—— *On the Genealogy of Morality*. Trans. Maudemarie Clark and Alan J. Swenson. Indianapolis: Hackett Publishing Company, Inc., 1998.

Orwin, Donna Tussing (ed.). *The Cambridge Companion to Tolstoy*. Cambridge: Cambridge University Press, 2002.

—— *Tolstoy's Art and Thought 1847–1880*. Princeton: Princeton University Press, 1993.

Parini, Jay. *The Last Station*. New York: Henry Holt, 1990.

Pascal, Blaise. *Oeuvres complètes*. Paris: Gallimard, 2000.

Poe, Edgar Allan. *Poetry and Tales*. New York: The Library of America, 1984.

Rosen, Stanley. *Metaphysics in Ordinary Language*. New Haven: Yale University Press, 1999.

Rousseau, Jean-Jacques. *The Discourses and Other Early Political Writings.* Ed. and Trans. Victor Gourevitch. Cambridge: Cambridge University Press, 1997.

Sade, D. A. F. de. *Philosophy in the Boudoir.* Trans. Joachim Neugroschel. New York: Penguin, 2006.

Sankovitch, Natasha. *Creating and Recovering Experience: Repetition in Tolstoy.* Stanford: Stanford University Press, 1998.

Scanlon, James. "Tolstoy among the Philosophers: His Book *On Life* and Its Critical Reception." *Tolstoy Studies Journal.* 15 (2006) 52–69.

Schaeffer, Jean-Marie. *Art of the Modern Age: Philosophy of Art from Kant to Heidegger.* Trans. Steven Rendall. Princeton: Princeton University Press, 2000.

Schelling, F. W. J. *Ausgewählte Schriften.* Ed. Manfred Frank. 6 vols. Frankfurt am Main: Suhrkamp Verlag, 1985.

—— *Philosophical Investigations into the Essence of Human Freedom.* Trans. Jeff Love and Johannes Schmidt. Albany: State University of New York Press, 2006.

Schmitt, Carl. *The Concept of the Political.* Trans. George Schwab. Chicago: University of Chicago Press, 1996.

Schopenhauer, Arthur. *The World as Will and Representation.* Trans. E. F. J. Payne. 2 vols. New York: Dover, 1966.

Shklovsky, Viktor. *Theory of Prose.* Trans. Benjamin Sher. Norman: Dalkey Archive Press, 1991.

Steiner, George. *Tolstoy or Dostoevsky: An Essay in the Old Criticism.* 2nd edn. New Haven: Yale University Press, 1996.

Strauss, Leo. *On Plato's "Symposium".* Chicago: The University of Chicago Press, 2001.

Tacitus. *Annals.* Trans. Alfred John Church and William Jackson Broddribb. New York: The Modern Library, 1942.

Troyat, Henri. *Tolstoy.* Trans. Nancy Amphoux. New York: Doubleday & Company, 1967.

Turgenev, Ivan S. *Polnoe sobranie sochinenii i pisem.* Moscow-Leningrad: Nauka, 1964.

Turner, C. J. G. "Tolstoy's *The Cossacks*: The Question of Genre." *Modern Language Review.* 73 (1978) 563–72.

Velkley, Richard. *Being After Rousseau: Philosophy and Culture in Question.* Chicago: The University of Chicago Press, 2002.

Walicki, Andrzej. *A History of Russian Thought from the Enlightenment to Marxism.* Trans. Hilda Andrews-Rusiecka. Stanford: Stanford University Press, 1979.

Wasiolek, Edward. *Tolstoy's Major Fiction.* Chicago: The University of Chicago Press, 1978.

Weisbein, Nicolas. *L'évolution religieuse de Tolstoï.* Paris: Librairie de Cinq Continents, 1960.

Wilde, Oscar. *The Picture of Dorian Gray.* Ed. Michael Patrick Gillespie. New York: W. W. Norton & Company, 1988.

Wilson, A. N. *Tolstoy.* New York: Fawcett Columbine, 1988.

Wittgenstein, Ludwig. *Philosophical Investigations.* New York: Macmillan Publishing Co., 1953.
—— *The Big Typescript: TS 213.* Ed. and Trans. C. Grant Luckhardt and Maximilian A. U. Aue. Malden: Blackwell Publishing, 2005.
Žižek, Slavoj. *Looking Awry: An Introduction to Jacques Lacan through Popular Culture.* Cambridge, Mass.: The MIT Press, 1991.
—— *Organs without Bodies: Deleuze and Consequences.* New York: Routledge, 2003.

FURTHER READING

WORKS BY TOLSTOY

There are several marvelous works of fiction not discussed in this book that I strongly recommend. The third large novel, *Resurrection* (1899), is seriously underrated and eminently worth reading on its own terms. Among the shorter works I recommend *Childhood* (1852), *The Sebastopol Sketches* (1855–1856), *Three Deaths* (1859), *Family Happiness* (1859) as well as two powerful late works dealing with sexual temptation, *The Devil* (1889) and *Father Sergius* (1898). A brilliant diatribe, "After the Ball" (1903), is typical of the late style, at once dense and limpid, as is another striking, longer work, *The Forged Coupon* (1902–1904).

Of the plays I recommend "The Power of Darkness" (1887), "The Fruits of Enlightenment" (1890) and "The Living Corpse" (1900).

Finally, I recommend the two-volume edition of Tolstoy's diaries edited by R. F. Christian.

SECONDARY READING

The recommendations I make below are confined to major secondary works available in English. For the interested reader, however, almost all the most significant secondary works available in Russian, or other languages, are identified in the works I do mention.

General

A particularly enjoyable overview of Tolstoy's works—unfortunately rather hard to find—is Pietro Citati's *Tolstoy*. Another, more polemical one is George Steiner's *Tolstoy or Dostoevsky: An Essay in the Old Criticism*. The two best scholarly introductions to Tolstoy are Richard Gustafson's *Leo Tolstoy: Resident and Stranger* and Donna

Orwin's *Tolstoy's Art and Thought 1847–1880*. Orwin's *Cambridge Companion to Tolstoy* is also well worth consulting. I strongly recommend any of Boris Eikhenbaum's extensive writings on Tolstoy that have been translated, like *The Young Tolstoi, Tolstoi in the Sixties* and *Tolstoi in the Seventies*.

As a general reference, I recommend *The Tolstoy Studies Journal*, which allows one to get a sense of where Tolstoy studies are at the moment as well as providing much useful bibliographical information.

Biography

There is no first-rate biography of Tolstoy in English, at least none in any way comparable to Joseph Frank's mammoth work on Dostoevsky. In absence of such a work, either A. N. Wilson's or Henri Troyat's *Tolstoy* provide serviceable reportage. Much more interesting, however, are Gorky's *Reminiscences of Tolstoy* and Bunin's *The Liberation of Tolstoy: A Tale of Two Writers*. Bunin's work is of particular value due to its astuteness and abundance of anecdotal information about the late Tolstoy.

Novels

Despite the importance of the novel for Tolstoy, there are surprisingly few general treatments of Tolstoy's relation to that genre. One is left with Bayley's *Tolstoy and the Novel*, which, despite many excellent discussions, stays too comfortably within the parameters of rather suspect critical models. Among general surveys of Tolstoy's novels, Wasiolck's *Tolstoy: The Major Fiction* is the most incisive, compact, and suggestive.

The best critical work on Tolstoy's novels deals with one or the other of the two great novels. For *War and Peace*, there are three essential works in English: R. F. Christian's *Tolstoy's "War and Peace,"* Sir Isaiah Berlin's incredibly influential essay, "The Hedgehog and the Fox," and Gary Saul Morson's provocative *Hidden in Plain View: Narrative and Creative Potentials in "War and Peace."* For *Anna Karenina*, one should consult Amy Mandelker's *Framing Anna Karenina: The Woman Question and the Victorian Novel* and, especially, Vladimir Alexandrov's *Limits to Interpretation: The Meanings of "Anna Karenina."* A more general introduction is provided by

FURTHER READING

Gary Saul Morson's recent *"Anna Karenina" in Our Time*. Eikhenbaum's two studies, mentioned above, *Tolstoi in the Sixties* and *Tolstoi in the Seventies*, give extremely valuable accounts of the development of both novels.

The "Shorter" Works

The late short works have become increasingly frequent topics of scholarly discussion. One recent and general study is Kåre Johan Mjør's *Desire Death and Imitation*. Otherwise, one would do well to consult specific studies, such as Gary Jahn's *The Death of Ivan Ilich: An Interpretation*, or articles, like those included in Michael Katz's translation, *Tolstoy's Short Fiction*.

Christian Works

The books by Gustafson and Orwin mentioned above are the proper places to start. Orwin provides the necessary account of Tolstoy's thought prior to his so-called conversion and Gustafson guides one through the Eastern Orthodox elements of Tolstoy's Christianity, his adherence to and rebellion from that tradition, with impressive thoroughness and clarity.

Walicki's *A History of Russian Thought from the Enlightenment to Marxism* is another useful work, setting out the contexts in which Tolstoy's religious thought emerges.

Philosophy

Tolstoy's complicated relation to the philosophical tradition and to philosophy in general has been treated best by Orwin. Gustafson's book is, again, another useful resource. Tolstoy has still not received the attention he deserves as a thinker. As a result there is a paucity of works specifically devoted to that theme other than those I have already mentioned. While Eikhenbaum gives a very useful account of Tolstoy's philosophical and mathematical interests while completing *War and Peace* and working through *Anna Karenina*, the distinctively philosophical aspects of the fiction have also been neglected. Garl Saul Morson's works on the great novels are a notable effort to offset this neglect.

172

Influence

A wonderfully accessible guide to Tolstoy's influence in the twentieth century is Steve Marks's chapter on Tolstoy in his *How Russia Shaped the Modern World: From Art to Anti-Semitism, from Ballet to Bolshevism*.

INDEX